INFLUENCES

INFLUENCES
Voices of Creative Dissent

Colin Ward

GREEN BOOKS

A Resurgence Book
First published in 1991 by
Green Books
Ford House, Hartland
Bideford, Devon
EX39 6EE

Set in Garamond 11 on 13½ by
Chris Fayers
Soldon, Devon
EX22 7PF

Printed by Biddles Ltd
Guildford, Surrey

Printed on recycled paper

British Library Cataloguing in Publication Data
Ward, Colin
Influences: voices of creative dissent
I. Title
824.914
ISBN 1-870098-43-9

CONTENTS

INTRODUCTION   7

1   EDUCATION
    William Godwin (1756-1836) and
    Mary Wollstonecraft (1759-1797)   13

2   POLITICS
    Alexander Herzen (1812-1870)   49

3   ECONOMICS
    Peter Kropotkin (1842-1921)   65

4   SOCIETY
    Martin Buber (1878-1965)   79

5   ARCHITECTURE
    William Richard Lethaby (1857-1931)
    and Walter Segal (1907-1985)   91

6   PLANNING
    Patrick Geddes (1854-1932)
    and Paul Goodman (1911-1972)   103

REFERENCES   133

READ FOR YOURSELF:
A bibliographical appendix   141

A LAST WORD   147

BY THE SAME AUTHOR

Anarchy in Action
Streetwork: The Exploding School (with Anthony Fyson)
Vandalism
Tenants Take Over
Housing: An Anarchist Approach
The Child in the City
Art and the Built Environment (with Eileen Adams)
Arcadia for All (with Dennis Hardy)
When We Build Again
Goodnight Campers! (with Dennis Hardy)
Chartres: The Making of a Miracle
The Allotment: Its Landscape and Culture (with David Crouch)
The Child in the Country
Undermining the Central Line (with Ruth Rendell)
Welcome, Thinner City: Urban Survival in the 1990s
Images of Childhood (with Tim Ward)
Talking Houses

Introduction

P EOPLE HAVE BEEN on our planet for a very long time and it is certain that none of us would have lasted without the influence of others. Those of us who survived did so because of the accumulated folklore and science of midwifery. The fact that we are still here is the result of endless influences which transcended nationality and ideology.

When I was 15 or 16 I read the *Daily Mirror* and copied down some words of that paper's columnist Cassandra (Bill Connor). In 1942, in the darkest and most bellicose days of the second world war, he chose to remind readers of the unseen influences that preserve us all:

> Our children are guarded from diphtheria by what a Japanese and a German did. They are saved from smallpox by an Englishman's work. They are saved from rabies because of a Frenchman. From birth to death they are surrounded by an invisible host—the spirits of men who never served a lesser loyalty than the welfare of mankind.[1]

I have always cherished this comment, partly because it rises above any kind of political, nationalistic or religious separatism, but also because it is a reminder that we are surrounded by endless strong and persuasive influences which tell us otherwise. All over the world people are willing to die, and to kill others, for the sake of some ideological or religious loyalty. Behaviour which would be unthinkable in their personal lives is seen as sanctified in eliminating the lives of others. Of all the unacceptable truths of the twentieth century, the century of total war and mass extermination as public policy, the fact we find hardest to swallow is that all the way down the pyramid of tyranny, the people who carried out campaigns of genocide were usually model citizens, devoted husbands and gentle fathers. All we can say of them is the same trite comment that we make about little local juvenile delinquents: they had fallen under bad influences.

But good people too can be bad influences. In the late 1930s poets with generous impulses would write poems urging others to go and fight to save the Spanish Republic. Young men, looking for a cause to serve went to Spain and died. Many decades later the surviving poets looked back with tolerant amusement at the romantic illusions of their youth. Those young men they influenced stay dead and forgotten. The same thing can be seen in all the other wars of the century, except that I cannot remember any figure worthy of anyone's respect in the United States and the Soviet Union attempting to influence opinion in favour of intervention in Vietnam or Afghanistan. They did not need to. The young men sent to kill and be killed were conscripts, and their opinions were irrelevant. Policy was made in secret by the military and political establishments feeding the population with lies and deliberately concocted misinformation.

How can such evil influences possibly gain their hold on any nation? The answer is that from infancy we are all influenced to adopt the habit of obedience to authority, whether it is that of parents, teachers, religious leaders, employers and the rulers of the state. The nation, the flag, the faith, our nearest and dearest, are in peril and our highest duty is to defend them against the enemy out there.

This is why I value most those quiet voices of dissent and scepticism, questioning the automatic inescapable influences all around us. I am just like anyone else. I have absorbed endless influences: personal and family contact, the example of others, oratory (always an influence to be wary of) and the written word. As a writer and propagandist I find myself endlessly quoting other people, usually because they express what I think or feel far better than I could myself. Not without misgivings I have narrowed down my own major influences to a handful of people, each of whom addresses one or other of the issues and dilemmas that interest me.

Anyone who writes a book of any kind, however mild or gentle, turns private thoughts into public statements and picks up some sort of obligation to readers, whether wanted or not. No-one has explained this better than Richard Hoggart, describing how a poor young man landed on his doorstep as a result of words he had written:

> He was clearly my responsibility not just as another human being in need but because he had been moved to seek me out by the effect some writing of mine had had on him; in particular by the chapter 'Scholarship Boy', about intellectual and emotional problems in adolescence, in *The Uses of Literacy*. I realised then more sharply than before that to write about inner problems of personality (to write about a great many other things too) is to issue an invitation on your own charity to those who read you. You are not free to push the writing out into the open water and disown it; it is always registered back to you at your intellectual address, a judgment by and on you.[2]

Hoggart is making a sobering and important point. Before you start trying to influence people, think about the consequences if your influence actually works. I'm reminded of the remark by Henry Miller in the prologue to the film *Reds*. 'All these people busy changing the world,' he complained, 'they couldn't even change themselves.'

I have certainly experienced the Hoggart effect myself. In the 1960s Penguin Books started its Education division, and in the 1970s, under new ownership, shut it down. It produced some brilliantly innovative series of school books. Among them was the *Connexions* series, edited by Richard Mabey, intended to entice reluctant readers of 14 upwards. He entrusted to me two of the most awkward topics, the book on *Violence* and the one on *Work*. They were widely used and were reprinted by Penguin every year all through the 1970s. I used to claim that my Work book was the only honest school book about work that by that time had been written.

Years later I had a letter from a reader. He had read that book, not as a schoolchild but as an employed adult. It had changed his life, he said, and he had never worked since. Should I have been gratified or horrified? He meant of course, that he had ceased to be employed by somebody else and was working for himself and his family. But suppose he had read it, under some kind of compulsion at school. Writers tend to be resourceful and adaptable. Readers could be anyone. Should the former seek to influence the latter by inciting a course of action which is appropriate for some but could be disastrous for others? Or do we all possess a mental filtering device which sifts out suggestions which do not speak to our condition?

Personally, I have been endlessly lucky with influences. I left school at fifteen and consequently was not told what to read. Other writers chanced to lead me to them. My choice of influences is like anyone's choice in music, the result of trial and error and much listening.

But it does interest me that any student today in half a dozen humanities subjects could go through a three year course with reading lists as long as your arm without learning of the existence of any of my influences. I take a certain satisfaction in the fact that this was always so. There is a long tradition in English literature that was ignored by the educated and by the patronage of the wealthy: you can pick out great names at random—Bunyan, Defoe, Blake, Cobbett.

On the other hand it is also true that today we have all totally forgotten a whole succession of books which were immensely influential. Two hundred years ago every radical thinker in Britain was reading the book known as Volney's *Ruins*,[3] and a hundred years ago their successors were reading Winwood Reade's *The Martyrdom of Man*. Endless biographies and autobiographies testify to the formative influences of these two books in shaping the way in which people came to terms with the world. In our own century there is similar testimony to the popular works of H.G. Wells or Bertrand Russell.

Long before the advent of scholarly paperbacks you could see on the shelves of humble but learned people, their prized accumulation of books in series like the Thinker's Library, the Home University Library and Everyman's Library. The first two of these were the most impressive, just because scholars had been persuaded to address an ordinary public in simple language. Richard Hoggart, once again, stresses the importance of that *haute vulgarisation* which, as he says, 'the French respect and the British fear.'[2]

My influences sought as wide an audience as possible. They did not all write particularly well, but they did address the reader as a serious person to be debated with, not as an ignoramus to be bullied or hectored. Still less did they pander to or flatter the prejudices or superstitions of their prospective readership. My major influences founded no parties. None of them started wars nor took part in governments. None of them inspired other people to hate each other. All were utter failures in the entrepreneurial culture. But in my experience not a day passes when I fail to recall the influence of one or another of them, whether I am thinking about education, the organisation of work, about architecture and planning, the right use of land or of our inheritance of human resourcefulness and natural resources.

The presentation that I make here of my accumulation of influences is partial. William Godwin and Mary Wollstonecraft, for example, were respectively, philosophers of politics and feminism. I choose to discuss them as educators. Martin Buber was a theologian. I expound him here as a sociologist. Paul Goodman saw himself as a poet and novelist, dragged by his sense of priorities into becoming a social critic. I choose to stress the ideas he developed, not on his own, but with his brother Percy. The advantage of being influenced by wide-ranging thinkers is that we can pinpoint selectively those aspects of their ideas that address the questions we actually ask ourselves.

I have quoted at length from my influences, without any apology. As a writer I know the book trade and local libraries very well. Consequently I know how unlikely it is that you will come into contact with the writers who have influenced me. The less the likelihood, the more I quote. I want to lure you into the discovery of the people who have influenced me for the most obvious of reasons: I want to share my pleasure. It would be gratifying to me if I managed to introduce you to a bunch of sympathetic people you might not have come across and would enjoy reading. This is why, when I look around my own bookshelves, I often can't actually find the works that I want to quote. I must have thrust them into other people's hands in the hope that this particular influence would rub off on them.

This is precisely my wish in regard to this book. Don't ignore my bibliographical appendix. It is one of the glories of our version of civilisation that, if you allow them time enough, any public library anywhere, and the library of any educational institution, from primary school to university, will, through inter-library loans, borrow every scrap of printed matter for you. This is a seldom-celebrated triumph of the instinct of mutual aid over the dogma of market forces. It enables all of us to share our own influences with everyone else.

Colin Ward

1

Education

William Godwin (1756-1836)
and
Mary Wollstonecraft (1759-1797)

E VERY ONE OF US has been a child, most of us become parents, while an astonishing number of us become, in some guise or other and at some time in our lives, teachers. Consequently many of us construct some kind of educational philosophy. But a sad number of teachers do not. They teach, not in the methods they were supposed to absorb in college, but in the ways that they themselves were taught at school.

This has sad results in an educational system closely related to social class. For thousands of Welsh children, for example, were urged out of a life in the pit or as a miner's wife, by their parents' ambitions for them, into the grammar school and teacher training college. Later, everywhere, with widening career horizons, and university opportunities, the renamed colleges of education were the fallback for those who had not attained anything that was thought 'better'. So the lower streams of the grammar schools provided the teachers who were to be exposed to the lower streams of non-academic children, but used the teaching methods which hadn't succeeded much with them. In the days when secondary modern schools have become comprehensive schools, and when colleges of education have become colleges of higher education, we have still not outgrown this survival of inappropriate teaching styles.

But of course plenty of people are influenced by some inspiring teacher they themselves encountered, or else by one of the great educators they have learned and read about: Pestalozzi or Froebel, or the nursery education pioneer Margaret McMillan, or a more recent educational experimenter like A. S. Neill. Neill was an educational failure, to the mortification of his parents: his father was the village schoolmaster. At the age of almost 14, not being good enough to go on to the Forfar Academy, he was sent to work, but was sacked both from the gas-meter firm and the draper's. He returned at 15 to become a pupil-teacher at his father's school. 'It's about all he's fit for,' said his despairing parents. I met and, like everyone else, relished Neill, but for my choice of educational influences I have to go back to the eighteenth century, to select William Godwin and Mary Wollstonecraft. You can search the histories of education for their names and you won't very often find them. They could even be called a husband-and-wife pair, but for the tragedy that their life together was a matter of months rather than years. She died in childbirth, and it is a sign of the unhealthy influence of narrowly literary history on the history of ideas, that for a long time the only significance of this pair was that their child was Mary Shelley, wife of the poet and author of *Frankenstein*.

Both my educational thinkers were vilified for a century. Writers on the period took over the tone of contemporary critics in describing Wollstonecraft as 'a hyena in petticoats' or a 'philosophical wanton'. Godwin was characterised as a 'cold rationalist' or as a sanctimonious sponger. (A 'venerable horse-leech' is the phrase used by Sir Leslie Stephen in the *Dictionary of National Biography*.) Their works were unread.

Character assassination is nothing new, but I had the luck to be introduced to them both by H. N. Brailsford's brilliant little book *Shelley, Godwin and their Circle*, first published in the Home University Library in 1913, and long out of print. I can remember my excitement when George Woodcock's *William Godwin: A Biographical Study* appeared in 1946. He had been denied access to the mountain of primary material known as the Abinger archive, now in the Bodleian Library at Oxford, which consists of the papers of Godwin, Wollstonecraft, Shelley, Mary Shelley and their family entanglements. Scholars like Peter Marshall, William St Clair and Richard Holmes have worked their way through these papers, overturning the accepted historical assessment of Godwin, while a new generation of feminists, seeking out their precursors, have rediscovered Wollstonecraft.

When I was finally able to borrow and copy passages from Godwin's school prospectus and to read beyond the opening sentence of his educational essay, *The Enquirer*, 'The true object of education, like that of every other moral process, is the generation of happiness,' I felt that I had come across an approach to childhood that I could agree with. I found that the same intense *empathy* with the child permeates Mary Wollstonecraft's writings. She was, as her editor Janet Todd stresses, 'first and last a writer on education'.

But judge for yourself their significance from my account of my educational influences.

In the City Road in London, just outside the boundary of the City itself (to avoid the limitations placed upon non-conformists) lies Bunhill Fields, the old Dissenters' Burying Ground, where, among forgotten thousands, are buried George Fox, John Bunyan, Daniel Defoe and William Blake. By the 1950s, decay, neglect and war damage had left it a wilderness of crumbling stones and open tombs.

My employer at the time was the landscape architect Peter Shepheard. He was commissioned to prepare plans for rehabilitating Bunhill Fields as a public garden. His scheme came to nothing because of disagreement between different interests as to which tombs should be retained, but in the course of his investigations he was lent a book of *Bunhill Memorials*, cataloguing the graves of several hundred dissenting ministers buried there, and describing their lives.

It became clear from these pious life-histories that with the penalisation of non-conformity, even the conservative wing of dissenters was driven into political radicalism in the long struggle for 'civil and religious liberty' (the words are always coupled in this way in the histories of dissent and in the epitaphs of its martyrs). Excluded by the Test Acts from the universities and from any kind of public office, they were equally critical of both Church and State.

The most striking thing, noted with disapproval by the anonymous compiler of the *Memorials* is the tendency, towards the end of the 18th century, for many of these dissenting ministers to move towards Deism (the search for a 'rational' religion) and Socinianism (unitarianism) and the rejection of the divinity of Jesus. The editor comments on the evolution of Joseph Priestley, the famous scientist, who 'passed through all the changes, from Calvinism to Arianism, then to Socinianism and finally to an Unitarian system perhaps, if possible, even lower than Socinianism'. He calls it, sarcastically, 'Dr Priestley's sliding-scale system'.

This was precisely the evolution of William Godwin. He was born at Wisbech in Cambridgeshire in 1756, the son and grandson of dissenting ministers. His grandfather and his tutors at the Dissenting Academy at Hoxton are buried at Bunhill Fields, and he himself became a dissenting minister until 1782, when he left his ministry at Stowmarket after a dispute with his congregation. His own account of his movement along Priestley's sliding scale was this:

> Till 1782 I believed in the doctrine of Calvin... The *Systeme de la Nature* (of d'Holbach), read about the beginning of that year, changed my opinion and made me a Deist. I afterwards veered to Socinianism, in which I was confirmed by Priestley's *Institutes*, in the beginning of 1783. I remember having entertained doubts in 1785, when I corresponded with Dr Priestley. But I was not a complete unbeliever till 1787.[1]

Rational non-conformity was linked, not only with political radicalism, but with scientific enquiry and technical innovation. Jacob Bronowski, in his life of William Blake, notes that 'The mining engineers, the textile inventors, the potters, the instrument makers, the ironmasters, were nearly all dissenters. Most of Blake's fellow artists were dissenters... The dissenting academies were the best scientific schools of the century and stood above the universities... The dissenting tradition proved its firmness of thought in the American war, and held it beyond the French Revolution. The Friendly societies and the craft unions of dissenting workmen made the core of the Corresponding Societies.'[2] This is the tradition to which Godwin belongs: the fruitful union of English dissent and the French enlightenment.

Godwin spent five years at the Hoxton Academy, a very thorough education, but his school life was a typical vignette of the earnest efforts of these humble nonconformists. He was first sent to a dame school. The woman who ran it died when he was eight and he then went to a school at Hindolveston with thirty boarders and seventy day-boys, conducted by a remarkable journeyman tailor called Akers. At the age of eleven he was sent to become the only pupil of Samuel Newton, an Independent minister at Norwich, Calvinist in religion and radical in politics. On one occasion, because of William's 'complacency', Newton beat him, to his pupil's intense amazement and indignation, which even his absurdly pompous description of the event does not entirely obscure:

It had never occurred to me as possible that my person, which hitherto had been treated by most of my acquaintances, and particularly by Mrs Sothren and Mr Akers, who had principally engaged my attention, as something extraordinary and sacred, could suffer such ignominious violation. The idea had something in it as abrupt as a fall from heaven to earth.[3]

At fifteen Godwin left Newton and returned to his former school to act as usher for Mr Akers for about a year. There is a relevant reflection in one of his essays:

> Convert one young person into a sort of superintendent and director to his junior, and you will see him immediately start up into a species of formalist and pedant. He is watching the conduct of another; that other has no such employment. He is immersed in foresight and care; the other is jocund and careless, and has no thought of tomorrow. But what is most material, he grows hourly more estranged to the liberal sentiments of equality, and inevitably contracts some of the vices that distinguish the master from the slave.[4]

When Godwin lost his religious faith he returned to London to earn a precarious living as a political journalist. But he first tried unsuccessfully to start a school. 'I actually hired a furnished house for the purpose,' he later explained, 'and published a pamphlet in recommendation of my plan: but I never secured a sufficient number of pupils at one time to induce me to enter upon actual business.'[5]

This was *An account of the Seminary that will be opened on Monday the Fourth Day of August, at Epsom in Surrey, for the Instruction of Twelve Pupils in the Greek, Latin, French and English Languages*, published in 1783 by T.Cadell in the Strand, 'of whom information respecting other particulars may be received.' It is certainly unusual as a school prospectus since it tells parents very little about the proposed curriculum beyond the information in the title. He begins in fact by comparing government and education, as 'the two principle objects of human power' and finds education to be the more important:

> The state of society is incontestably artificial; the power of one man over another must be always derived from convention, or from conquest; by nature we are equal. The necessary consequence is, that government must always

depend upon the opinion of the governed. Let the most oppressed people under heaven once change their mode of thinking, and they are free... Government is very limited in its power of making people either virtuous or happy; it is only in the infancy of society that it can do anything considerable; in its maturity it can only direct a few of our outward actions. But our moral dispositions and character depend very much, perhaps entirely, upon education...

He goes on to pay tribute to Rousseau's educational treatise *Émile*, but criticises his system for its 'inflexibility', and then attacks the conventional education of his day:

Modern education not only corrupts the heart of our youth, by the rigid slavery to which it condemns them, it also undermines their reason, by the unintelligible jargon with which they are overwhelmed in the first instance, and the little attention that is given to accommodating their pursuits to their capacities in the second.

A small school, like the one he proposed to establish, is preferable both to a large one and to a solitary education, because of the advantages of a social community, though not for the spirit of competition, instead of which, 'I would wish to see the connection of pupils consisting only of pleasure and generosity. They should learn to love and not to hate each other.' The child should not be motivated to study through fear, nor even through hope of reward, but through the intrinsic attraction of the way in which the subject is presented. Godwin rejected the physical and moral coercion of the child whose natural dignity and candour were precious assets to be kept intact. It is not surprising that he failed to attract enough parents to open the school. No other school prospectus before or since contained a sentence like his observation that 'There is not in the world a truer object of pity than a child terrified at every glance and watching with anxious uncertainty the caprices of a pedagogue.'[6]

Setting up house in London as a writer, his only regular source of income came from a solitary pupil, the only paying pupil he ever had. This was a boy called Willis Webb, an orphan sent to him by his old tutor at Hoxton, Dr Kippis. Godwin's first biographer, Kegan Paul, having seen the subsequent correspondence between Godwin and Webb, commented that 'The letters show that Godwin was able to inspire genuine enthusiasm in the young... and they are the first instance of the way in which he was considered one to whom the young might resort as to an oracle.' His second pupil was more difficult. He was a twelve year old boy, Tom Cooper, a distant relative, orphaned in 1787, for whom Godwin, in spite of his own poverty, provided a home from 1788 to 1792. Mary Shelley noted, in the material she gathered for a never-written book about her father, that Tom was 'a spirited boy, extremely independent and resolute, proud, wilful and indolent' and his relationship with Godwin was tempestuous. Cooper took to the stage and eventually became famous as an actor in America. He continually expressed his indebtedness to his teacher. Godwin, during the years with Cooper, would note in his diary his own failings as a teacher. 'Is not his temper embittered by sternness, i.e. over-exactness in lessons and propensity to play the censor on trivial occasions? Let me, then, aim at gentleness, kindness, cordiality.' Many years later, in 1812, he wrote to Shelley:

> I have again and again been hopeless concerning the children with whom I have voluntarily, or by the laws of society, been concerned. Seeds of intellect and knowledge, seeds of moral judgment and conduct, I have sown; but the soil for a long time seemed ungrateful to the tiller's care. It was not so; the happiest operations were going on quietly and unobserved, they unfolded themselves to the delight of every beholder.[7]

After Tom Cooper, Godwin may not have sought any more pupils, but they certainly sought him. Clever young men and women sought him out for the sheer brilliance and erudition of his philosophical writings and, even though his life was beset by financial problems and domestic tragedies, were treated with endless kindness. Even in his neglected old age, 'Caroline Norton, Sheridan's grand-daughter, was the last in a succession of young women, beautiful and brilliant, ready to come to the aid of the master.'[8] As H.N. Brailsford remarked, 'He practised what he preached, and he would himself give with a generosity which seemed prodigal, to his own relatives, to promising young men, and even to total strangers. He supported one disciple at Cambridge, as he had educated Cooper in his younger days.'[9]

Mary Wollstonecraft came from a quite different background from Godwin's. His family were sober nonconformists, frugal and reverencing moral probity and education. Her father had 'the tastes and vices of a country squire without the acreage or capital; he loved both horse and bottle but proved impatient and incompetent as a farmer.'[10] The grammar school was for her brother, but not for Mary and her sisters. She went to the village school.

> In fact she learned little more than reading and writing, but had enough wit to flourish under this sort of neglect; she wrote of village schools later with a glow of enthusiasm that suggests she enjoyed hers. Her religious indoctrination was mercifully deficient too, product of the sleepy Anglicanism of the times...[11]

Her passionate, tempestuous nature made her yearn for independence, and she adopted the only options available for the daughters of the impoverished, improvident gentry: lady's companion, teacher in tiny girls' schools, governess. And, like Godwin, she had the good fortune to fall into the orbit of Joseph

Johnson, the radical dissenting publisher who gave her a £10 advance for her book *Thoughts on the Education of Daughters*. She wrote it in six weeks in 1786. Johnson published it and sought more work from her, the novel *Mary*, and a children's book of *Original Stories from Real Life*.

It was the French Revolution that profoundly changed the lives of both William and Mary. In 1789, at the Meeting House in Old Jewry, Dr Richard Price, Unitarian minister and scientist, preached his sermon congratulating the French on 'the Revolution in that country and on the prospect it gives to the two first kingdoms in the world of a common participation in the blessings of civil and religious liberty'. Price's sermon was answered by Edmund Burke's *Reflections on the Revolution in France*, defending the established order, and this in turn evoked several radical counterblasts.

Mary wrote *A Vindication of the Rights of Men*, which was soon overshadowed by Tom Paine's magnificent *Rights of Man*. And William set about his monumental *Enquiry Concerning Political Justice*, which he intended should 'by its inherent energy and weight... place the principles of politics on an immovable basis.' The two met at a dinner party of Joseph Johnson's in 1791, invited to meet Paine. Godwin was to recall that 'the conversation lay principally between me and Mary. I, of consequence, heard her very frequently when I wished to hear Paine.'[12]

But Wollstonecraft's best biographer, Claire Tomalin, suggests that 'it is possible that Paine dropped into Mary's mind at about this moment the idea of a book on women's rights... why should Mary not produce a second Vindication for her own sex?'[13]

She wrote *A Vindication of the Rights of Woman* in six weeks. Editors invariably refer to its lack of structure, its rhetoric and its discursiveness, as though they were marking student essays. But it was William Godwin who, after its author's death only five years later, wrote an assessment of its historical significance that remains true two centuries later:

But when we consider the importance of its doctrines, and

the eminence of genius it displays, it seems not very improbable that it will be read as long as the English language endures. The publication of this book forms an epoch in the subject to which it belongs; and Mary Wollstonecraft will perhaps hereafter be found to have performed more substantial service for the cause of her sex, than all the other writers, male or female, that ever felt themselves animated by the contemplation of their oppressed and injured state.[14]

She did not set out to write an educational treatise, but since the education of girls, or the absence of it, were at the heart of the subjugation of women, she was bound 'to assert that till women are more rationally educated, the progress of human virtue and improvement in knowledge must receive continual checks. And if it be granted that woman was not created merely to gratify the appetite of man, or to be the upper servant, who provides his meals and takes care of his linen', it must follow that mothers and fathers should be concerned with other qualities in their daughters than 'a desire to please the sex on which they are dependent'.

The widely influential educational text of the period was Rousseau's *Émile*, and one of her tasks was to attack Rousseau's assumptions about the 'natural' girl:

To preserve personal beauty, woman's glory! the limbs and faculties are cramped with worse than Chinese bands, and the sedentary life which they are condemned to live, whilst boys frolic in the open air, weakens the muscles and relaxes the nerves. As for Rousseau's remarks, which have since been echoed by several writers, that they have naturally, that is from their birth, independent of education, a fondness for dolls, dressing, and talking—they are so puerile as not to merit a serious refutation. That a girl, condemned to sit for hours together listening to the idle chat of weak nurses, or to attend at her mother's toilet, will endeavour to join the conversation, is, indeed, very natural; and that she will imitate her mother or aunts, amuse herself by adorning her lifeless doll, as they do in dressing her, poor innocent babe! is undoubtedly a most natural consequence.

Warming to this point she writes devastatingly about the accidental advantages that accrued to girls who had *not* been educated:

I have, probably, had an opportunity of observing more girls in their infancy than J.J. Rousseau—I can recollect my own feelings, and I have looked steadily around me; yet, so far from coinciding with him in opinion respecting the first dawn of the female character, I will venture to affirm, that a girl, whose spirits have not been damped by inactivity, or innocence tainted by false shame, will always be a romp, and the doll will will never excite attention unless confinement allows her no alternative. Girls and boys, in short, would play harmlessly together, if the distinction of sex was not inculcated long before nature makes any difference—I will go further, and affirm, as an indisputable fact, that most of the women, in the circle of my observation, who have acted like rational creatures, or shewn any vigour of intellect, have accidentally been allowed to run wild...

She wants children to be 'natural', not in Rousseau's sense, but so as not to constrain 'the pure animal spirits, which make both mind and body shoot out, and unfold the tender blossoms of hope', but she believes in openness and honesty with the young:

That children ought to be constantly guarded against the vices and follies of the world appears to me a very mistaken opinion.

and she attacks 'the ridiculous falsities which are told to children, from mistaken notions of modesty... Children very early see cats with their kittens, birds with their young ones, etc. Why then are they not to be told that their mothers carry and nourish them in the same way?' And she attacks the values absorbed in the boarding schools of the affluent, whether for girls or boys.

> I should, in fact, be averse to boarding-schools, if it were for no other reason than the unsettled state of mind which the expectation of the vacations produces. On these the children's thoughts are fixed with eager anticipating hopes, for, at least, to speak with moderation, half of the time, and when they arrive they are spent in total dissipation and beastly indulgence.

And in one of those footnoted digressions of personal observation that irritate her editors, but bring her readers closer, she recalls:

> I went to visit a little boy at a school where young children were prepared for a large one. The master took me into the schoolroom, etc, but whilst I walked down a broad gravel walk, I could not help observing that the grass grew very luxuriantly on each side of me. I immediately asked the child some questions, and found that the poor boys were not allowed to stir off the walk, and that the master sometimes permitted sheep to be turned in to crop the untrodden grass. The tyrant of this domain used to sit by a window that overlooked the prison yard, and one nook turning from it, where the unfortunate babes could sport freely, he enclosed, and planted it with potatoes. The wife likewise was equally anxious to keep the children in order, lest they should dirty or tear their clothes.

Wollstonecraft believed that the liberation of both women and men demanded co-education, at all ages. 'Girls and boys still together? I hear some readers ask: yes. And I should not fear any other consequence than that some early attachment might take place; which, whilst it had the best effect on the moral character of the young people, might not perfectly agree with the view of the parents...' This is her formula, two hundred years old, for primary education:

> The school for the younger children, from five to nine years of age, ought to be absolutely free and open to all classes... The school-room ought to be surrounded by a large piece of ground, in which the children might be usefully exercised, for at this age they should not be confined to any sedentary employment for more than an hour at a time. But these relaxations might all be rendered a part of elementary education, for many things improve and amuse the senses, when introduced as a kind of show, to the principles of which, dryly laid down, children would turn a deaf ear. For instance, botany, mechanics, and astronomy. Reading, writing, arithmetic, natural history, and some simple experiments in natural philosophy, might fill up the day; but these pursuits should never encroach on gymnastic plays in the open air...[15]

Godwin, meanwhile, was labouring methodically on his *Political Justice*, arguing every point from first principles, in stately 18th century prose, sending each section to the printers while working on the next. The book appeared in February 1793, two months after Tom Paine had been sentenced to death in his absence on a charge of high treason for writing *The Rights of Man*. The response was immediate. William and Mary had both become famous overnight. It was, as William Hazlitt put it acutely, 'the very zenith of a sultry and unwholesome popularity': certainly it was too good to last, and was the prelude to years of calumny and neglect.

Godwin set out to write a philosophy of politics, ('a science,' he says in his preface, 'which may be said to be yet in its infancy') and since such a comprehensive programme must start from first principles and must rest on moral and psychological foundations, it is natural that his educational philosophy should find a place in his exposition. The first is his restatement of the 'nature versus nurture' debate. He wrestled with this issue in differing ways in successive editions of his book, but handled it better in his later educational writings. Education, he says, happens in three different ways. It happens by accident, it happens deliberately, and it happens because our ideas are modified by 'the form of government under which we live'.

It is all very well to have elaborate schemes of education, he suggests, but most people's experience is determined by lucky or unlucky accidents which have not entered into the teacher's plans:

> Two children walk out together. One busies himself in plucking flowers or running after butterflies, the other walks in the hand of their conductor. Two men view a picture. They never see it from the same point of view, and therefore strictly speaking never see the same picture. If they sit down to hear a lecture or any piece of instruction, they never sit down with the same degree of attention, seriousness or good humour. The previous state of mind is different, and therefore the impression received cannot be the same.

'If people's juvenile adventures had been more accurately recorded', Godwin argues, it would be found 'that the most trivial circumstance has sometimes furnished the original occasion of awakening the ardour of their minds and determining the bent of their studies.'

Then he approaches the share of political institutions and forms of government in the education of every human being. It is nearly impossible to 'oppose the education of the preceptor, and the education we derive from the forms of government under which we live' to each other. Firstly because, 'Should any one talk of rescuing a young person from the sinister influence of a corrupt government by the power of education, it will be fair to ask, who is the preceptor by whom this talk is to be effected? Is he born in the ordinary mode of generation, or does he descend among us from the skies? Has his character been in no degree modified by that very influence he undertakes to counteract?' As long as parents and teachers in general shall fall under the established rule, he declares, 'it is clear that politics and modes of government will educate and infect us all.' And secondly, 'supposing the preceptor had all the qualifications that can reasonably be imputed, let us recollect for a moment what are the influences with which he would have to struggle... Under a government fundamentally erroneous, he will see intrepid virtue proscribed, and a servile and corrupt spirit uniformly encouraged.'

It is here that Godwin diverges sharply from the philosophers of the French Enlightenment. Rousseau, Helvetius, Diderot and Condorcet all put forward schemes for national systems of education, postulating of course, an ideal state. But for Godwin an ideal state was a contradiction in terms, and his starting point was the distinction between society and government, felicitously phrased by Tom Paine:

> Society is produced by our wants and government by our wickedness; the former promotes our happiness positively by uniting our affections; the latter negatively by restraining our vices. The one encourages intercourse, the other creates distinctions. The first is a patron, the last a punisher. Society in every state is a blessing; but government even in its best state is a necessary evil.[16]

For Godwin it was an unnecessary evil, and his whole book was an elaborate argument for a non-governmental society. The major educational text in his day among progressive people was Rousseau's *Émile*. Although Rousseau postulates a completely individual education (human life is ignored and the tutor's entire time is devoted to poor Émile), he did, nevertheless, concern himself with the social aspect of educational organisation, arguing in his *Discourse on Political Economy* for public education 'under regulations prescribed by the government', since 'If children are brought up in common in the bosom of equality; if they are imbued with the laws of the State and the precepts of the General Will... we cannot doubt that they will cherish one another mutually as brothers... to become in time defenders and fathers of the country of which they will have been so long the children.'

Godwin, in his chapter 'Of National Education', adds a more cogent argument in its favour by putting the question, 'If the education of our youth be entirely confined to the prudence of their parents, or the accidental benevolence of private individuals, will it not be a necessary consequence, that some will be educated to virtue, others to vice, and others again entirely neglected?'

His answer is to put forward three kinds of objections to schemes for national education, so cogent that they merit quotation at length.

The injuries that result from a system of national education are, in the first place, that all public establishments include in them the idea of permanence. They endeavour, it may be, to secure and to diffuse whatever of advantage to society is already known, but they forget that more remains to be known... But public education has always expended its energies in the support of prejudice; it teaches its pupils not the fortitude that shall bring every proposition to the test of examination, but the art of vindicating such tenets as may chance to be previously established... This feature runs through every species of public establishment; and, even in the petty institutions of Sunday schools, the chief lessons that are taught are a superstitious veneration for the Church of England, and to bow to every man in a handsome coat... Refer them to reading, to conversation, to meditation, but teach them neither creeds nor catechisms, neither moral nor political...

Secondly, the idea of national education is founded in an inattention to the nature of mind. Whatever each man does for himself is done well; whatever his neighbours or his country undertake to do for him is done ill. It is our wisdom to incite men to act for themselves, not to retain them in a state of perpetual pupillage. He that learns because he desires to learn will listen to the instructions he receives and apprehend their meaning. He that teaches because he desires to teach will discharge his occupations with enthusiasm and energy. But the moment political institution undertakes to assign to every man his place, the functions of all will be discharged with supineness and indifference...

Thirdly, the project of a national education ought uniformly to be discouraged on account of its obvious alliance with national government. This is an alliance of a more formidable nature than the old and much contested alliance of church and state. Before we put so powerful a machine under the direction of so ambitious an agent, it behoves us to consider well what we do. Government will not fail to employ it to strengthen its hand and perpetuate its institutions... Their views as instigators of a system of education will not fail to be analogous to their views in their political capacity; the data upon which their conduct as statesmen is vindicated will be the data upon which their institutions are founded. It is not true that our youth ought to be instructed to venerate their constitution, however excellent; they should be instructed to venerate truth... (Even) in the countries where liberty chiefly prevails, it is reasonably to be assumed that there are important errors, and a national system has the most direct tendency to perpetuate those errors and to form all minds upon one model.[17]

Now why, at the end of the 20th century, do I stress those theoretical objections from the end of the 18th century? For the sound and simple reason that Godwin was unique among the philosophers of education in warning us against them.

In many countries the 'old and much contested alliance of

church and state' gave way to hard-won battles to exclude religious propaganda from state-funded schools, as in France or the United States. But in its stead, in every American school, the day begins with the ceremony of saluting the flag. In Britain, after decades of negotiation with rival Christian organisations, the Education Act of 1944 laid down that every school day should begin with a 'common act of worship'. Schools interpreted this clause liberally, conscious that we lived in a secular society as well as one with many different parental religious beliefs, only to be reminded by the Education Act of 1988 that the law meant what it said.

History tends to be written by people educated outside the state-funded education system, under a more liberal regime, but the growth of 'oral history' and the publication of humble people's recollections has revealed the degree of automatic indoctrination pervading the public education system. Empire Day was celebrated in British schools on May 24, to celebrate the British conquest of half the globe, while 'even in the petty institutions of Sunday schools', the pennies of poor children were gathered to enable rival bodies like the Church Missionary Society and the London Missionary Society to convert the Chinese, the Indians and Africans, as well as the inhabitants of the South Sea Islands to their rival versions of Christianity.

And as for deference to the Church of England and people in handsome coats, there is endless evidence from the last century and our own. Stan Holmes, a schoolboy in the 1930s, remembers how 'When the squire or farmer came along you had to stand and raise your hat to him. Same for the vicar and schoolmaster.'[18]

But the most devastating support for Godwin's warnings of the dangers of a 'national system' came as late as the 1980s, when the British government, despite its rhetoric about 'rolling back the frontiers of the state', decided to impose on all schools under local authority control, a National Curriculum. The Secretary of State for Education explained that, in history, 'the programmes of study should have at the core the history of Britain, the record of its past and, in particular, its political, constitutional and cultural heritage.' This unobjectionable statement hid the fact that there are many ways of interpreting British history. In the 1930s, one particular version of German history was required from every school in Germany as a national curriculum, so that in 1945 one of the unexpected tasks of the Allied Control Commission in Germany was to write new textbooks. For seventy years the history of the Soviet Union was rewritten to suit current versions of reality. The result was that in 1988 the school leaving examinations in history had to be cancelled, with the message from above that official versions of the past consisted of lies, distortions and omissions, while new texts had yet to be written as the amount of historical truth it was permitted to teach was continually expanding.

In Britain, when the working party appointed to report to one Secretary of State presented their findings to his successor, their report was rejected by the Prime Minister, as not 'national' enough.[19] Godwin's arguments remain important.

Godwin followed *Political Justice* with his novel *Caleb Williams*, intended to convey the same message to a different audience. Mary Wollstonecraft, meanwhile, was living through the aftermath of the revolution and the Terror. She had a protracted and painful affair with an American adventurer Gilbert Imlay, and a daughter, Fanny, by him. In pursuit of his business interests she made a journey to Scandinavia, which resulted in her *Letters Written during a Short Residence in Sweden, Norway and Denmark*. This is seen by its sympathetic modern editor Richard Holmes as 'the most imaginative English travel book since Sterne's *A Sentimental Journey*'. He also draws our attention to 'the pleasure with which she describes the sexual freedom of the young' in Scandinavia:

> Young people, who are attached to each other, with the consent of their friends, exchange rings, and are permitted to enjoy a degree of liberty together, which I have never noticed in any other country. The days of courtship are therefore prolonged, till it be perfectly convenient to marry: the intimacy

often becomes very tender: and if the lover obtain the privilege of a husband, it can only be termed half by stealth, because the family is wilfully blind. It happens very rarely that these honorary engagements are dissolved or disregarded.[20]

Her book appeared in 1796, after a second suicide attempt, the result of her desperate efforts to re-establish a relationship with Imlay. Then came the improbable romance, the unusual mix, people said, of 'fire and ice'. The passionate, tempestuous Mary and the restrained, logical William fell in love. In 1797 Mary died after the birth of their daughter Mary. What Richard Holmes calls 'a significant new marriage between Imagination and Reason' ended in personal tragedy. Godwin wrote a tender *Memoir* of her life and, to his mortification, readers found it shocking and disgusting. Holmes, who published it together with her travel book, suggests in his brilliant introduction that both are 'crucial documents of the historic moment of transition and the Romantic renewal of hope and feeling.'[21] I am sure he is right.

The rest of the family story is well known. Mary Godwin grew up to be Mary Shelley. Godwin married again and spent the rest of his life as an inpecunious educational publisher, supporting a large brood of other people's children, and 'was in practice the most careful, considerate, and loving of fathers'. Mary Wollstonecraft had been 'first and last a writer on education'[22] and after her death Godwin collected together her unfinished *Letters on the Management of Infants* and the other sad fragments she left behind.

He went on writing about education for the whole of his life, but the most absorbing of his reflections on education were published in his book *The Enquirer*, written during the months of his growing friendship with Mary. These essays were, he tells us, principally the result of conversations: 'The author has always had a passion for colloquial discussion' since 'there is a vivacity, and, if he may be permitted to say it, a richness in the hints struck out in conversation, that are with difficulty attained in any other method.'[23]

The tone is set by the first essay 'Of Awakening the Mind', which begins with a resounding affirmation:

> The true object of education, like that of every other moral process, is the generation of happiness.
> Happiness to the individual in the first place. If individuals were universally happy, the species would be happy.
> Man is a social being. In society the interests of individuals are intertwisted with each other, and cannot be separated. Men should be taught to assist each other. The first object should be to train a man to be happy; the second to train him to be useful, that is, to be virtuous.

To make a man virtuous, he goes on, 'we must make him wise', wisdom being 'not only directly a means to virtue; it is also directly a means to happiness.'

He still believes the child at birth to be an 'unformed mass' but immediately qualifies this. 'What may be the precise degree of difference with respect to capacity that children generally bring in the world with them, is a problem that is perhaps impossible completely to solve. But, if education cannot do everything, it can do much.'

In his essay 'Of the Sources of Genius' he returns again to the question of heredity and environment, and of innate differences, a question which, he says, 'has but lately entered into philosophical disquisition', it having previously been thought too obvious for controversy that genius is born and not made.

> Examine the children of peasants. Nothing is more common that to find in them a promise of understanding, a quickness of observation, an ingenuousness of character, and a delicacy of tact, at the age of seven years, the very traces of which are obliterated at the age of fourteen. The cares of the world fall upon them. They are enlisted at the crimping-house of oppression. They are brutified by immoderate and unintermitted

labour. Their hearts are hardened, and their spirits broken, by all that they see, all that they feel, and all that they look forward to. This is one of the most interesting points of view in which we can consider the present order of society. It is the great slaughter-house of genius and of mind. It is the unrelenting murderer of hope and gaiety, of the love of reflection and the love of life.

Godwin shares neither Rousseau's cult of the simple peasant and the noble savage, nor his anti-intellectualism. As an educational thinker he is whole-heartedly 'on the side of the child', but his feeling for childhood is completely untouched by Rousseau's sentimental nostalgia. The key to his attitude is to be found in a striking essay 'Of the Happiness of Youth.' He begins by challenging his reader's assumptions:

> A subject upon which the poets of all ages have delighted to expatiate, is the happiness of youth.
> This is a topic which has usually been handled by persons advanced in age. I do not recollect that it has been selected as a theme for description by the young themselves.
> It is easy to perceive why the opinion upon which it proceeds, has been generally entertained.
> The appearance of young persons is essentially gratifying to the eye. Their countenances are usually smooth; unmarked with wrinkles, unfurrowed by time. Their eye is sprightly and roving. Their limbs elastic and active. Their temper kind, and easy of attachment. They are frank and inartificial; and their frankness shows itself in their very voice. Their gaiety is noisy and obtrusive. Their spirits are inexhaustible; and their sorrows and their cares are speedily dismissed.
> Such is frequently the appearance of youth. Are they happy? Probably not.
> A reasonable man will entertain a suspicion of that eulogium of a condition, which is always made by persons at a distance

from it, never by the person himself.
I never was told, when a boy, of the superior felicity of youth, but my heart revolted from the assertion. Give me at least to be a man!'

And he goes on in this vein to set out the grievances of childhood:

Children, it is said, are free from the cares of the world. Are they without their cares? Of all cares, those that bring with them the greatest consolation are the cares of independence. There is no more certain source of exultation than the consciousness that I am of some importance in the world. A child usually feels that he is nobody. Parents, in the abundance of the providence, take good care to administer to them the bitter recollection. How suddenly does a child rise to an enviable degree of happiness, who feels that he has the honour to be trusted and consulted by his superiors?

But of all the sources of unhappiness for the young, the greatest, he says, is a sense of slavery. 'How grievous the insult, or how contemptible the ignorance, that tells a child that youth is the true season of felicity, when he feels himself checked, controlled, and tyrannised over in a thousand ways... There is no equality, no reasoning, between me and my task-master. If I attempt it, it is considered a mutiny. If it be seemingly conceded, it is only the more cutting mockery. He is always in the right; right and power in these trials are found to be inseparable companions... Dearly indeed, by twenty years of bondage, do I purchase the scanty portion of liberty, which the government of my country happens to concede to its adult subjects!'
And yet it would be unjust to think that the pains inflicted by adults on the young are the result of malice: 'they are the fruits of tenderness and disinterested zeal.' But these are 'in a great measure nugatory, where the methods pursued are founded in error. If the condition of the young is to be pitied, the condition

of those who superintend them, is something equally worthy of compassion.'

The intention of Godwin's speculations, he says, should be regarded 'as that of relieving, at once, the well-meaning but misguided oppressor, *and* the unfortunate and helpless oppressed.' He makes the same point about his approach to education. Our 'animadversions' must be directed against the instructor and not against his pupil, for the simple reason that 'The pupil is the clay in the hands of the artificer; I must expostulate with *him*, not with his materials. Books of education are not written to instruct the young how they are to form their seniors, but to assist the adult in discovering how to fashion the youthful mind.'

There is a reverence, Godwin argues, 'that we owe to every thing in human shape. I do not say that a child is the image of God. But I do affirm that he is an individual being, with powers of reasoning, with sensations of pleasure and pain, and with principles of morality; and that in this description is contained abundant cause for the exercise of reverence and forbearance.' And he argues that violence towards children is a mirror of violence in society and between nations:

Violate not thy own image in the person of thy offspring. That image is sacred. He that does violence to it is the genuine blasphemer. The most fundamental of all the principles of morality is the consideration and deference that man owes to man; nor is the helplessness of childhood by any means unentitled to the benefit of this principle. The neglect of it among mankind at large, is the principal source of all the injustice, the revenge, the bloodshed and the wars, that have so long stained the face of nature.

The object of harshness is intended to be 'to bring the delinquent to a sense of his error'. But, says Godwin, 'It has no such tendency. It simply proves to him, that he has something else to encounter, beside the genuine consequence of his mistake; and that is that there are men, who, when they cannot convince by reason, will not hesitate to overbear by force. Pertinacious and persuaded as he was before in the proceeding he adopted, he is confirmed in his persuasion, by the tacit confession which he ascribes to your conduct, of the weakness of your cause.'

This argument occurs in the essay on 'Cohabitation'—the general theme of which is the 'excess of familiarity' which results from continual and close contact. ('Every man has his ill humours, has fits of peevishness and exacerbation. It is better that he should spend these upon his fellow beings or suffer them to subside of themselves?') He illustrates his contention by asking us to imagine that instead of our own child we substitute 'a child with whom we have a slight acquaintance, and no vicious habits of familiarity.' Here is a situation known to every parent:

> ... I would then ask any man of urbane manners and a kind temper, whether he would endeavour to correct the error of this stranger child, by forbidding looks, harsh tones and severe language? No; he would treat the child in this respect as he would an adult of either sex. He would know that to inspire hatred to himself and distaste to his lesson, was not the most promising road to instruction. He would endeavour to do justice to his views of the subject in discussion; he would communicate his ideas with all practicable perspicacity; but he would communicate them with every mark of conciliation and friendly attention. He would not mix them with tones of acrimony, and airs of lofty command. He would perceive that such a proceeding had a direct tendency to defeat his purpose.

Let it be supposed, Godwin urges us in the next essay 'Of Reasoning and Contention' that a parent

> ... accustomed to exercise a high authority over his children, and to require from them the most uncontending submission,

has recently been convinced of the impropriety of his conduct. He calls them together, and confesses his error. He has now discovered that they are rational beings as well as himself, that he ought to act the part of their friend, and not of their master; and he encourages them, when they differ in opinion with him as to the conduct they ought to pursue, to state their reasons, and proceed to a fair and equal examination of the subject.

If this is to be of any use, he argues, it must be to a *real* discussion 'that they are invited, and not to the humiliating scene of a mock discussion. The terms must be just and impartial.' But what usually happens is for the parent to say, 'No, I have heard you out; you have not convinced me; and therefore nothing remains for you but to submit.' Putting himself in the place of the child, Godwin replies, 'Upon these terms I cannot enter the lists with you. I had rather a thousand times know at once what it is to which I must submit, and comply with a grace, than to have my mind warmed with the discussion, be incited to recollect and to state with force a whole series of arguments, and then be obliged to quit the field with disgrace...'

He concludes that 'Where the parent is not prepared to grant a real and *bona fide* equality, it is of the first importance that he should avoid the semblance of it... The situation I deprecate is that of a slave, who is endowed with the show and appearance of freedom.' Here he is speaking the language, not of a disingenuous 18th century theorist like Rousseau, but of a 20th century practitioner like David Wills. He was a Quaker I knew and respected, who spent his working lifetime in the trouble-laden task of running residential homes for delinquent boys and girls, sent to him by the courts. David wrote in his book *Throw Away Thy Rod*:

I have frequently referred with contempt to the arrangement whereby some well-meaning adult (I *think* such people are well-meaning) will say, 'Now then, children. Let's all have a meeting and decide to do so-and-so.' I call that bogus and dishonest, because the adult does not really intend to permit free discussion and a free decision... This is the sort of person who will say, as a member of the Underwood Committee said to me, 'I tried it, but it didn't work.' Of course it didn't work, and the more intelligent the children the sooner it fails.'[24]

Godwin's comment on this issue is that 'The way to avoid this error in the treatment of youth is to fix in our mind those points from which we may perceive that we shall not ultimately recede, and whenever they occur, to proscribe them with mildness of behaviour, but with firmness of decision. It is not necessary that in so doing we should really subtract anything from the independence of youth. They should no doubt have a large portion of independence; it should be restricted only in cases of extraordinary emergency; but the boundaries should be clear, evident and unequivocal.' David Wills again, with a similar intellectual honesty, makes the same point in his account of *The Barns Experiment*:

It is better to limit the sphere of the children's responsibilities to something very small, if that authority is absolute, than to give them a wide but vague sphere of control with the danger that you might step in one day and veto a decision that they have made. But you will find, if you have confidence in them, that you are repeatedly being astonished by their wisdom.[25]

Godwin concludes his approach to this theme with the thought that 'It is not necessary that, like some foolish parents, we should tenaciously adhere to every thing that we have once laid down, and prefer that heaven should perish rather than we stand convicted of error. We should acknowledge ourselves fallible; we should retract unaffectedly and with grace whenever we find that we have fallen into mistake.' Once again, the sentiment, if not the language, has a modern ring. Paul and Jean Ritter in their book *The Free Family* remark on how much simpler and friendlier relations are when we admit frankly that we are just as prone to error as they are:

> Children who have long known that everybody is silly sometimes, that others have reasons for being silly just as they have themselves, can understand the difficulties of a teacher surprisingly well. The result, we have found, is a degree of co-operation in class which is normally only associated with that bred by great fear of punishment. That this is the outcome of self-regulation never ceases to surprise people.[26]

What can be more unjust, Godwin asks in his essay on 'Frankness and Deception','than the conduct of those parents, who, while they pride themselves in the ingenuity with which they deceive their children, express the utmost severity and displeasure when their children attempt a reprisal, and are detected in schemes of similar adroitness?' And he goes on to criticise Rousseau for the attitude of systematic deception which is the basis of *Émile*:

> Rousseau, to whom the world is so deeply indebted for the irresistible energy of his writings, and the magnitude and originality of his speculations, has fallen into the common error in the point we are considering. His whole system of education is a series of tricks, a puppet-show exhibition, of which the master holds the wires, and the scholar is never to suspect in what manner they are moved. The scholar is never to imagine that his instructor is wiser than himself. They are to be companions; they are to enter upon their studies together; they are to make a similar progress, it is to seem the pure effect of accident... The treatise of Rousseau upon education is probably a work of the highest value... But in the article here referred to, whatever may be its merits as a vehicle of fundamental truths, as a guide of practice it will be

found to be of the most pernicious tendency. The deception he prescribes would be in hourly danger of discovery...

The revolution in attitudes to childhood which Rousseau initiated asserted the right of the child to be valued as a child and not as a diminutive or imperfect adult. Godwin values the child as a *person* who is a child and who will be an adult, and the question he raises in another essay is that of 'whether we should endeavour to diminish or increase the distinction between youth and manhood.' He begins by deprecating the 'kind of premature manhood' sometimes observed in the young, the 'pertness and primness' which are 'always in some degree ridiculous or disgusting in persons of infant years.' Robbed of the chief blessing of youth—'a thoughtless, bounding gaiety'—the premature adults have a forced and artificial behaviour. Certainly, they discuss and assert, 'but it is with a borrowed judgment'.

There is also an opposite type of character. 'The child is timorous and bashful, and terrified at the idea of encountering a stranger; or he will accost the stranger with an infantile jargon.' Godwin criticises those parents who encourage baby-talk and 'receive a kind of sensual pleasure from the lisping and half-formed accents of their children; and who will treasure and re-echo them...' There are children, he remarks, 'who seem as if it were intended that they should always remain children, or at least make no proportionable advances toward manhood. They know nothing of the concerns of men, the state of man, or the reasoning of man.'

What is really desirable, he thinks, is 'that a child should partake of both characters, the child and the man.' The hilarity of youth is 'too valuable a benefit, for any reasonable man to wish to see it driven out of the world'. In fact it would probably be 'cultivated by adults... and... even preserved into old age' were it not for a false ideal of decorum. But 'if hilarity be a valuable thing, good sense is perhaps still better.' A man can be useful, contented and happy without gaiety, but is hardly worthy of the name of man 'if seriousness be not an ingredient in his disposition'. This does not mean that we should 'check the sallies of youth', but we should tolerate them rather than foster them. 'Nothing is of worse effect in our treatment of the young or the old, than a continual anxiety, and an ever eager interference with their conduct.'

> The thoughts of childhood indeed, though to childhood they are interesting, are in themselves idle... But the period advances, in which the case is extremely altered. As puberty approaches, the turn which the mind of a young person shall then take, may have the most important effects upon his whole character. When his heart beats with a consciousness that he is somewhat, he knows not what; when the impatient soul spurns at that constraint, to which before it had submitted without a murmur; when a new existence seems to descend upon him, and to double all that he was before; who shall then watch his thoughts and guide his actions?

This is a time, says Godwin (like a thousand other writers on adolescence) 'when he is indeed in want of a pilot,' yet 'this is a time when of all others he shuns the confidence of his superiors.' Even if as a child he had been open and unreserved, now 'shame suspends the communication' and he dares not reveal 'his unfledged notions'. Instead he chooses as a confidant 'a person not less young, ignorant and inexperienced than himself' or else 'his confidant is of an imagination already debauched and depraved, who instead of leading him with safety through untried fields, perpetually stimulates and conducts him to measures the most unfortunate.' He is talking of course, about sexual experiment, and, in the oblique language of his times, he makes a plea for guidance and instruction rather than a conspiracy of silence.

The wise parent or teacher would seek 'by all honest arts' to be admitted to the confidence of youth, and we should understand that the way to gain anyone's confidence is to 'make ourselves as much as possible his equals, that our affection towards him should display itself in the most unambiguous colours, that we should discover a genuine sympathy in his joys and his sorrows, that we should not play the part of the harsh monitor and austere censor...'

Godwin, like Wollstonecraft, has a radical approach to the school:

> If a thing be really good, it can be shown to be such. If you cannot demonstrate its excellence, it may well be suspected that you are no proper judge of it... Is it necessary that a child should learn a thing, before it can have any idea of its value? It is probable that there is no one thing that it is eminently important for a child to learn. The true object of juvenile education is to provide, against the age of five and twenty, a mind well regulated, active, and prepared to learn. Whatever will inspire habits of industry and observation, will sufficiently answer this purpose. Is it not possible to find something that will fulfil these conditions, the benefit of which a child shall understand, and the acquisition of which he may be taught to desire? Study with desire is real activity: without desire it is but the semblance and mockery of activity. Let us not, in the eagerness of our haste to educate, forget all the ends of education.

He goes on to reiterate that 'the most desirable mode of education therefor, in all instances where it shall be found sufficiently practicable, is that which is careful that all the acquisitions of the pupil shall be preceded and accompanied by desire.' The best motive, 'less pure than the first, but not so displeasing as the last, which is desire, not springing from the intrinsic excellence of the object, but from the accidental attractions which the teacher may have annexed to it.' Once again he is reflecting a very common experience.

As a final sample of Godwin's vision of the transformation of the school, one which completely contradicts current educational wisdom, reflect on this conclusion:

According to the received modes of education, the master goes first, and the pupil follows. According to the method here recommended, it is probable that the pupil should go first, and the master follow... The first object of a system of instructing, is to give the pupil a motive to learn. We have seen how far the established systems fail in this office. The second object is to smooth the difficulties which present themselves in the acquisition of knowledge... This plan is calculated entirely to change the face of education. The whole formidable apparatus which has hitherto attended it, is swept away. Strictly speaking, no such characters are left upon the scene as either preceptor or pupil. The boy, like the man, studies, because he desires it. He proceeds upon a plan of his own invention, or which, by adopting, he has made his own. Everything bespeaks independence and equality. The man, as well as the boy, would be glad in cases of difficulty to consult a person more informed than himself. That the boy is accustomed almost always to consult the man, and not the man the boy, is to be regarded rather as an accident, than anything essential. Much even of this would be removed, if we remembered that the most inferior judge, may often by the varieties of his apprehension, give valuable information to the most enlightened...

I have quoted at great length from *The Enquirer* for the very good reason that Godwin's book is so hard to find that my extracts will be for most readers a substitute for finding a library with a copy of the book itself. Its educational essays are the most radical ever written. They make nonsense of the notion that child-centred schooling and the appreciation of children as persons in their own right and for their own sake are twentieth-century inventions. Don't read too much into Godwin's use of male nouns and pronouns throughout: it was, like his language, the habit of the time.

The warmth of these essays owes much to Mary. They were

written in that happy year when 'as they were both writing for a living, they regularly exchanged manuscripts for criticism,' and he gave a touching account of the way in which 'her taste awakened mine' and 'her sensibility determined me to a careful development of my feelings.' In the second edition of his *Memoir*, he was to write:

> Mary and myself perhaps each carried farther than to its common extent the characteristic of the sexes to which we belonged. I have been discouraged, when casting the sum of my intellectual value, by finding that I did not possess, in the degree of some other persons, an intuitive sense of the pleasures of the imagination... What I wanted in this respect, Mary possessed in a degree superior to any other person I ever knew. Her feelings had a character of peculiar strength and decision; and the discovery of them, whether in matters of taste or of moral virtue, she found herself unable to control... A companion like this, excites and animates the mind...[27]

The psychological honesty of this opinion, supported by modern biographers of both of them, lends force to his eulogy of Mary as a teacher:

> With children she was the mirror of patience... Her heart was the seat of every benevolent feeling; and accordingly, in all her intercourse with children, it was kindness and sympathy alone that prompted her conduct. Sympathy, when it mounts to a certain height, inevitably begets affection in the person towards whom it is exercised; and I have heard her say that she never was concerned in the education of one child, who was not personally attached to her, and earnestly concerned not to incur her displeasure. Another eminent advantage she possessed in the business of education, was that she was little troubled with scepticism and uncertainty...[28]

Now we live in a time of immense scepticism and uncertainty about education. For decades, education was oversold. Every increase in student numbers at the upper and more expensive end of the system, every new development in educational technology was a step towards some great social goal. There was an inevitable backlash which blamed the education system for the decline of British manufacturing industry and sought to turn the school system into a nursery of market entrepreneurialism. I rejoice in having discovered long ago my major educational influences, William and Mary, whose approaches to the child and to the school belong to a different style of educational aspirations.

2

Politics

Alexander Herzen
(1812-1870)

M Y EDUCATIONAL THINKERS, Godwin and Wollstonecraft, were
poised at that moment in history which we characterise as
the romantic revolution. Their most sensitive editor, Richard
Holmes, explains that the work of their small circle of beleaguered
radicals, 'was a kind of culmination: a consecration of that New
Sensibility in which the rational hopes of the Enlightenment were
catalysed by that element of imagination and personal rebellion
which we now know as Romanticism'.[1]

My major political influence, Alexander Herzen, was seen by his
biographer, E.H. Carr, as the product of the Romantic revolution,
and the tragedies of his family life (like those of the complex
brood of other people's children for whom Godwin was the
breadwinner) were presented as the consequence of the cult of
personal feeling and fulfilment, regardless of the effect on others.
I read Carr's book *The Romantic Exiles: a Nineteenth-Century
Portrait Gallery* in the 1940s with enormous enjoyment. As one
of its characters was Michael Bakunin, it led me to buy Professor

Carr's subsequent biography of him too. And it led me to buy Constance Garnett's translation of Herzen's superlative book *My Past and Thoughts*. (This was at Bumpus's bookshop in Oxford Street, London, and those little green volumes, believe it or not, had been on the shelves since the 1920s in their white paper jackets. One of the changes about the book trade that we never mention is that books used to have an infinitely longer 'shelf-life' than they do today.) Later I became severely critical of Carr's approach. He is deliciously ironical about both Herzen and Bakunin, but you could close his books without the slightest indication that they were both important political thinkers, almost alone in predicting the evolution of twentieth-century totalitarianism.

I was alerted to Herzen's real significance by an essay of George Woodcock's in his book *The Writer and Politics*, published in 1948, and by an article in the American journal *Politics*, published in New York in the 1940s and distributed in Britain by Freedom Press. Its editor was the dissident journalist Dwight Macdonald, who had a series called 'Ancestors', because he was looking, all those years ago, for the point where the ideology of the political left went wrong. I mention all this bibliographical trivia just to push home the point that good ideas and timely evaluations come from the way-out and unsuccessful fringes of journalism, not from the commercially viable centre. But what confirmed for me the importance of Herzen as a political influence was the series of lectures on 'A Marvellous Decade' given in London in 1954 by Isaiah Berlin, and broadcast on what was then the BBC Third Programme that year. Two years later, Berlin introduced an English version of Herzen's essays on *The Russian People and Socialism* and *From the Other Shore*. If you want to understand the disaster of the aftermath of the Russian revolution, and its devastating effect on other twentieth-century revolutions, read it.

Herzen is a sparklingly acute and witty political mentor. His views link directly with those of William Godwin, when he chances to write about childhood. 'What is the purpose of a child?'

he asks. And he answers, 'We think that the purpose of a child is to grow up, simply because it does grow up. But its purpose is to play, to enjoy itself, to be a child. If we merely look to the end of the process, the purpose of all life is death.'

This is simply an incidental exposition of the idea that Isaiah Berlin calls Herzen's central political and social thesis, that 'one of the greatest of sins that any human being can perpetrate is to seek to transfer moral responsibility from his own shoulders to those of an unpredictable future order, and, in the name of something which may never happen, perpetrate crimes today which no one would deny to be monstrous if they were performed for some egoistic purpose, and do not seem so only because they are sanctified by faith in some remote and intangible Utopia.'[2]

In other words, Herzen's appeal is that he, a nineteenth-century polemical journalist, accurately anticipated the horrors of the twentieth century. But it is more than that. He was a wonderfully acute observer of his own times and his rambling and discursive autobiography is one of the great masterpieces of Russian literature. Let's get to know him better!

In 1851 the Russian revolutionary Michael Bakunin, after having been chained to the wall of his cell and condemned to death for his part in the revolutions of 1848 in both Saxony and Austria, was handed over to Russian justice and imprisoned in the Peter-Paul fortress 'to rot indefinitely'. There, his biographer writes, 'the swollen, flabby figure with toothless jaw and unkempt beard bore now little resemblance to the sturdy, rather dandified young giant who had entered the Saxon prison; and a glimpse in a mirror made him recoil from himself in horror'. From his cell he had, at the request of the Emperor Nicholas I, written a *Confession*, thirty thousand words long, which is probably in its mixture of fulsome self-abasement, incredible frankness and unrepentant defiance, the most extraordinary autobiographical fragment in the Russian language. Nicholas wrote on the first page a note for his son and heir, later

Alexander II: 'It is worth your while to read this—it is very curious and instructive.'

In this document, which was not made public until 1921, Bakunin had two requests. One was that he might be taken out of solitary confinement in the fortress; the other was that he might be permitted to see his family for one last time. For, as E.H. Carr wrote, the landscape of Premukhino—the long, low, roomy eighteenth-century house in its estate 'of five hundred souls' about fifteen miles north-west of Moscow—carried a store of memories shared by the Bakunin family,

> and Michael, in the darkest moment of his career, could still conjure out of the distant past the winding Osuga; the water-meadows and the little island where they had played in the middle of the pond; the old sawmill with the miller fishing in the mill stream; the early morning pilgrimages through the garden while the spiders' webs were still hanging on the leaves; the moonlight walks in spring, when the cherry-blossom was in flower and brothers and sisters would sing *Au clair de la lune* in chorus; the solemn burial of Varvara's pet sparrow, for which Borchert, the German tutor, composed an epitaph; the winter readings of *The Swiss Family Robinson* round the hearth—everything that was summed up for a Bakunin in the golden word Premukhino.[3]

These memories epitomise our Western picture of Russian landed society before the revolution, which is drawn not only from the wonderful flowering of novels and plays in the nineteenth century, but from the rich stream of personal memoirs, particularly of childhood and youth, covering the century from Aksakov to Gorky, with an ample harvest in the last doomed decades of Imperial rule from Pasternak, Paustovsky and Nicolas Nabokov. They evoke a world of birch trees, governesses, samovars, sailor suits and sleigh-rides, with, in Gabriele Annan's words, 'the taste of tea and jam sharpened and sweetened by the sense of the vast empty steppes beyond the garden and the imminent end of it all'. For most of these recollections, though not all, are those of members of the aristocracy.

In this rich literature there are three masterpieces, and it cannot be coincidental that each is by a man who, like Bakunin, spent much of his life attempting to destroy the foundations of the feudal autocracy into which he was born. These are Alexander Herzen's *My Past and Thoughts*, Leo Tolstoy's fictionalised trilogy *Childhood, Boyhood and Youth*, and Peter Kropotkin's *Memoirs of a Revolutionist*. These men belonged to different generations (Herzen was born in 1812, Tolstoy in 1828, and Kropotkin in 1842); they never met (apart from a brief encounter in London between Herzen and Tolstoy, which the latter remembered vividly nearly fifty years later) but their lives were intertwined through common friendships with other writers like Turgenev and the exiled mathematician Peter Lavrov, through common concern with the abolition of serfdom and in further social change, and through avid reading of each other's works.

Herzen, Bakunin, Tolstoy and Kropotkin were four sons of the Russian nobility, gifted, eager and passionate, who were faced with the central question that Imperial Russia posed for all the intelligent children of its ruling elite. We are growing up, they could not avoid perceiving, into an oriental despotism, terrifyingly strengthened by Prussian militarism and overlaid with a veneer of French culture. The atmosphere, once we have moved beyond the joys of childhood, is stifling. How should we live? *What is to be done?* This question was the title of a drearily didactic but immensely influential novel by Chernyshevsky, and a whole generation of educated young people modelled their lives upon those of its characters. When Turgenev made the nihilist Bazarov the hero of *Fathers and Sons* there were impassioned discussions and quarrels about the veracity of the character and of Turgenev himself. For just as the men and women who peopled the great novels were regarded as though they were living beings whose dilemmas and choices were those facing the readers of the books, so those four men seemed larger than life in the answers they gave to the questions posed to Russians of the privileged classes in the nineteenth century. (Bakunin indeed served as the model not only for Turgenev's Rudin, but for Dostoevsky's Stavrogin. Tolstoy himself provided one fictional self-portrait after another: young Nikolenka Irtenyev, Pierre Bezukhov, Konstantin Levin.) The four men were great archetypes of response to the inevitability of revolution.

When did the revolution become inevitable? In retrospect it was as long ago as 1826, with the execution of the five Decembrists, hanged for their part in the plot of December 1825 to overthrow the autocracy and establish constitutional government. Nicholas I, in signing the death warrant for Pestel, Ryleyev, Kakhovsky, Bestuzhev and Muraviev-Apostol, signed the death warrant of the Romanov dynasty. Alexander Herzen and his lifelong friend the poet Ogarev were boys at the time. They climbed the Sparrow Hills (now the Lenin Hills) outside Moscow. 'Flushed and breathless, we stood there mopping our faces. The sun was setting, the cupolas glittered, beneath the hill the city extended farther than the eye could reach; a fresh breeze blew on our faces, we stood leaning against each other and, suddenly embracing, vowed in sight of all Moscow to sacrifice our lives to the struggle we had chosen.'

It was a gesture characteristic both of their youth and of the romantic era, but decades later, after both had been filled with domestic tragedies and when both were exiles in England, Herzen dedicated *My Past and Thoughts* to Ogarev with the words:

> Life... lives, peoples, revolutions, beloved faces have appeared, changed and vanished between the Sparrow Hills and Primrose Hill... Everything round me is changed: the Thames flows instead of the Moscow river, and I am surrounded by a strange people... and there is no more a way for us back to our

country... only the dream of two boys, one of thirteen, the other of eleven, has remained intact!

Herzen's book, which he began in the 1850s and to which he added further parts until his death at the age of fifty-eight in 1870, increasingly conscious that he was providing an account, not just of his own life, but of his country and his century, is the ideal rambling and discursive masterpiece to be stranded with on a desert island. Isaiah Berlin is right to see it as 'one of the great monuments to Russian literary and psychological genius'. This is apparent from the very first pages, where Herzen recounts the story, told him frequently by his old nurse, of his own adventures as a babe-in-arms during the French occupation of burning Moscow, and his father's unexpected role as a messenger between Napoleon and the Tsar. We could be reading *War and Peace*, and indeed that novel's author, who declared that he had never met another man 'with so rare a combination of scintillating brilliance and depth', drew upon Herzen's pages for significant detail.

Quite apart from all its other virtues, his book is an innoculative antidote for anyone who, faced with the devastating history of the Russian empire in the twentieth century, imagines that there was any hope from the previous regime. In 1762, a century before the emancipation of the serfs, the Russian gentry were freed from their feudal obligation to serve the Empress. Alexey Alexandrovich Jakovlev, director of the Imperial Mint, belonged to a family that had provided administrators for successive tsars and emperors for centuries, but his four sons were among the first generation of those 'superfluous men' who fill the pages of the Russian novels of the following century. Spendthrift, cultivated and cosmopolitan, no longer obliged to pursue a career in the service of the autocracy, they wasted their lives in the social round, in idleness and apathy, or in the cynical philandering mirrored in Mozart's operas.

The four brothers all resigned their military commissions early. The eldest, as related in Martin Malia's account of Herzen's family history, seduced a Swedish governess who bore him three children, while 'to ensure the woman's dependence on him, he destroyed her passport, and she passed the rest of her days without any legal identity, completely at the mercy of his caprice.' The second returned to his country estate 'where his cruelty towards the peasants and his lechery with their daughters provoked a reaction from which he barely escaped with his life. Returning to Moscow, he passed the remainder of his life between his library and the harem of serf women, in loneliness, 'idleness and endless lawsuits'. The third brother 'sired a number of servile bastards, who seem to have grown up in obscurity among his peasants as if they were not his children, but who at least escaped the more tragic lot of some of their cousins'.[4]

The youngest of the brothers, Ivan Alexeevich, left the army in 1801 and spent the next ten years wandering around western Europe. Before his departure he had fathered a son by a peasant girl. During his absence his sister, Princess Khovansky, felt impelled to rescue the boy from serfdom, and brought him up. When Ivan Alexeevich returned from Europe in 1811, she presented him with his ten-year-old son. According to Herzen's cousin, Tatiana Passek, 'the father, glancing at the boy, put his hand on his shoulder, coldly kissed him, and turning to his sister, expressed, in French, his displeasure that she had taken on herself the education of the child without consulting him.'

In his travels in Europe Ivan Alexeevich had met a fifteen-year-old girl from Stuttgart, Luiza Haag, who returned with him, pregnant, to Moscow as war became imminent. There, early in the fatal year 1812, she gave birth to a son, Alexander Ivanovich, who was given the surname Herzen, either cynically, because he was a 'love child' or affectionately, because he was the 'child of his father's heart'. Certainly Yakovlev was, in his morose and remote way, as indulgent to Alexander as he was brutal towards the unwanted Yegor.

Herzen's conclusion about his father's generation could have been spoken by Turgenev or, half a century later, by Chekhov: 'In Russia, men who were exposed to the influence of this powerful European current did not make history, but they became unlike other men. Foreigners at home and foreigners abroad, spoilt for Russia by European prejudices and for Europe by Russian habits, they were a living contradiction in terms and sank into an artificial life of sensual enjoyment and monstrous egoism.' The child Shushka, as he was known, had more than the usual share of juvenile egoism himself. Adored by all, he was endlessly spoilt by the servants of the household, pampered, but isolated from companions of his own age, except for the servant children, whom he dominated just as their own parents were dominated by his. The only children of his own age and social class who were admitted to the household were his cousins, and they became precious to him.

The first was the delightful Tatyana, five years older than Shuska, who was the granddaughter of the eldest of the Jakovlev brothers, and was parked successively, like an awkward piece of family furniture, in the various Jakovlev households. Whenever she came to the gloomy mansion he was overjoyed. Together they exalted over Rousseau's *Confessions* and Goethe's *Elective Affinities*, and he was desolated when she left. Then into his life came another, more distant cousin, 'Nick' Ogarev, another lonely and gifted boy, whose life ever afterwards was inextricably linked with Herzen's. They too read together, and were intoxicated by the dramas of Schiller. They were thrilled by the story of *William Tell*, and identified with the anarchic outlaws of *The Robbers* and with the friendship of Carlos and Posa in *Don Carlos*.

Yet another lonely cousin was Natalya Zakharin, daughter of the second of the Yakovlev brothers and one of his serfs. She, too, had been adopted by Princess Khovansky, but there was little affection in her gloomy, tear-stained childhood. Some of Herzen's bitterest pages described Natalya's early years and the way in which 'loneliness and harsh treatment at the tenderest age left a black trace on her soul, a wound which never fully closed.'

His own bookish isolation ended dramatically when, at seventeen, he entered Moscow University, an institution, which, he explained, was far more open and democratic than its English counterparts. His studies, the discovery of new intellectual worlds, the comradeship of his fellow students, were bound to lead him into membership of a *kruzhok*, or circle, of like-minded people, and in Russian history the 'circle of Herzen and Ogarev' is always counterposed to that of Stankevich, which included such figures as Belinsky and Bakunin.

Inevitably, in the political climate of Russia, such circles were watched, spied upon, and if possible, infiltrated by the police and their agents. Herzen and Ogarev were arrested, imprisoned, tried and sentenced to that peculiarly Russian institution of administrative exile. The second volume of his memoirs is one of the great classics of the enormous literature of the Russian penal system. 'From the nursery I had passed into the lecture-room, and from the lecture-room to a small circle of friends, an intimate world of theories, dreams and without contact with practical life; then came prison, with its opportunities for reflection; and contact with life was only beginning now and here, over the ridge of the Ural Mountains.'

He was beginning what he saw as the life of a hermit, but 'a hermit thoroughly in love'. For in 1838, hearing that Princess Khovansky was proposing to mary off Natalya to an unsought admirer, he travelled to Moscow on a false passport and eloped with her to Vladimir. When he was at last permitted to return, his father was able to get him appointed to a civil service job in St Petersburg, but in less than a year he was dismissed and banished to Novgorod. Ultimately he resolved, if he could get a passport, to leave Russia. The disssident 'circles' were splitting apart, his father had died, and he was consumed by that implacable hatred of the autocracy of Nicholas I which led him years later, when the news came of the Tsar's death, to give sixpences to the bewildered urchins of Twickenham to cry in the streets 'Hurrah! Zarnicoll is dead!'

The next step in both his personal and political life is graphically described in the opening paragraph of Carr's account of the romantic exiles:

On Sunday, 19 January 1847, a party of travellers left Moscow in two carriages padded, for protection against the winter cold, with fur. The party consisted of ten persons: Alexander (or Sasha for short) aged seven, Kolya aged three, a deaf-mute, and Natalie the younger, commonly called Tata, aged two; Herzen's mother, Luiza Haag; two female friends and dependents of the family; a Baltic German named Karl Sonnenberg, who had been imported years ago from Reval to be Herzen's tutor, and who now acted as major-domo of his household; and a children's nurse. The terms of Herzen's passport, which was good for six months, showed that he was travelling with his family, for the sake of his wife's health, to Germany and Italy.[5]

None of them was ever to return. Herzen's mother and younger son died in 1851 when a steamer sank in the Mediterranean. His wife died in the following year after a disastrous *affaire* with the German poet Herwegh. Herzen himself became a wanderer around western Europe. Even in his thirteen years of residence in England he had at least fifteen different addresses in London and its suburbs. (He used to declare that he could find his way around any English house blindfold.)

In the tidal wave of revolution that swept across the continent in 1848 he was a passionate observer, closely associated with the anarchists Bakunin and Proudhon, with whom he shared an absolute iconoclasm and an insistence on the importance of personal liberty, which was not generally shared by the revolutionaries of his day, or ours. His epitaph on the hopes and disappointments of that year was the magnificent collection of essays, *From the Other Shore*. This is, as Isaiah Berlin remarks, 'a frontal attack upon the doctrine at that time preached by almost every left-wing orator in Europe (with the notable exception of Proudhon, Stirner and a handful of anarchists to whom no one listened) about the sacred human duty of offering up oneself—or others—upon the altar of some great moral or political cause— some abstract principle or abstract noun capable of stirring strong emotion, like Nationality, or Democracy, or Equality, or Humanity, or Progress.'[6]

From the Other Shore, however closely it was linked to the events that Herzen witnessed in Italy and France, still has its splendidly-phrased political message for every twentieth-century zealot, prepared to sacrifice his generation for the sake of *his* version of the future:

> If progress is the end, for whom are we working? Who is this Moloch who, as the toilers approach him, instead of rewarding them, only recedes, and as a consolation to the exhausted, doomed multitudes crying 'We, who are about to die, salute thee', can give back only the mocking answer that after their death all will be beautiful on earth. Do you truly wish to condemn all human beings alive today to the sad role of caryatids supporting a floor for others some day to dance on... or of wretched galley slaves, up to their knees in mud, dragging a large barge filled with some mysterious treasure and with the humble words 'Progress in the Future' inscribed on its bows? An end that is infinitely remote is not an end, but a trap; an end must be nearer—it ought to be, at the very least, the labourer's wage, or pleasure in the work done. Each age, each generation, each life had and has its own fullness...[7]

In 1851, the year of his personal tragedies, he wrote a celebrated essay on *The Russian People and Socialism*, which took the form of an open letter to Jules Michelet, who had bitterly attacked the Russian oppression of Poland. Herzen, who was always a champion of the Poles, urges Michelet not to confuse the Russians with their government. The Slav peoples, he argues, have never believed in the centralised state, and their natural form of expression is in federalism. He sees in the ancient communal institutions of the Russian people, the *mir* or village commune, and the *artel* or artisan's co-operative, not the mainstay of feudal tradition, which is how in his view the Slavophiles saw them, but the basis of a popular revolution, more lasting, more rooted in reality, than the conspiracies of professional revolutionaries.

It is on the instinctive Russian socialism that we have to build, he argues, bringing from the West, not bourgeois revolutions and parliamentarism, but western ideas of individual freedom and advanced agricultural techniques. 'Work, active work,' he cries, 'on behalf of the Russian people, which has laboured enough on our behalf!' In these ideas he was anticipating the *narodnik* or Populist movement of later decades.

For Herzen, the first task was to work for the emancipation of the serfs. 'We are slaves, because we are masters,' he wrote, 'we are ourselves serfs because we keep others in servitude.' In London he started the Russian Free Press, the first uncensored printing in the Russian language. The success of the pamphlets which were smuggled into Russia led him to publish first an annual, *The Pole Star,* which bore on its cover the portraits of the Decembrists executed by Nicholas I, and then, when Ogarev had joined him in 1856, his famous periodical *The Bell* (*Kolokol*). 'Between 1857 and 1861,' wrote David Mirsky, '*The Bell* was the principal political force in Russia. It was read by everyone and not least by those in power.' Another literary historian, Marc Slonim, declares that it was 'the accepted mouthpiece of Russian public opinion, and nobody saw anything paradoxical in the fact that it came from London and a group of émigrés.'[8]

This extraordinary achievement was partly due to the sparkling wit coupled with both passion and erudition that pervades Herzen's journalism, just as it runs all through the memoirs, and partly because he had an excellent network of informants, enabling him to expose abuses and name names. From a series of villas in Westbourne Park, Richmond, Fulham and Putney High Street, he became one of the most influential men in Russia. As another account says, 'He kept track as accurately of the corruption and cruelties of the most insignificant police officer as he did of the transactions in the Senate and Council chamber. The dread of appearing in *Kolokol* soon paralysed the hand of the boldest and most hardened officials in the service.' But *The Bell* also had a positive programme, intended to appeal to all progressive opinion, demanding an end to serfdom, the abolition of corporal punishment and of the censorship.

At length, in 1861, the new Tsar, Alexander II, signed the decree emancipating the serfs. It was the crowning moment of Herzen's public life, and he held a celebration for all the Russian exiles at his house in Paddington, but on that very evening the news came through that Russian troops were firing on rioters in Warsaw. 'Only forty days!' wrote Herzen in *The Bell*. 'Why did not *this man* die on the day when the liberation manifesto was published to the Russian people?'

The legal emancipation of the peasantry was not followed by measures for their economic liberation, and the régime of Alexander hardened into the same repressive autocracy as that of his ancestors. Herzen's influence declined. He would not give up his support for the insurrectionary Poles, and those Russian liberals whose liberalism did not extend to subject peoples turned away from *The Bell*. The new generation of revolutionaries also turned against him, for he offered no simple, clear-cut solution.

Meanwhile, Bakunin had re-emerged, bursting into Herzen's house in Paddington in 1861 with the question 'Can one get oysters here?' In spite of his *Confession*, he had not been released from solitary confinement, but in March 1854 he was transferred from the Peter-Paul fortress to the Schlusselberg prison. In 1857 Alexander II gave Bakunin the choice of remaining there or of perpetual banishment to Siberia. He chose Siberia and escaped by way of Yokohama, San Francisco and New York. After the collapse of the Polish uprising, he began to elaborate his collectivist anarchist theories and became Marx's bitter opponent in the First International. Anyone reading his voluminous fragmentary writings will find them full of uncannily accurate prophesies of the nature of the Marxist dictatorships of the twentieth century.[9]

Herzen, Bakunin and Ogarev moved their press to Geneva in an effort to win the support of the exiled Russian revolutionaries there. With misgivings Herzen supported the secret society 'Land and Liberty', but in 1867 he ceased to publish *The Bell* and three years later he died. 'What an astonishing writer!' Tolstoy remarked three years later. 'If his works were not forbidden to the young, our whole life of the last twenty years would have been different.'[10]

In his last year, Herzen addressed to Bakunin his *Letters to an Old Comrade*. He agrees with Bakunin that the goal is 'the transformation of the bourgeois state into a folk-state', but he points out that the attitudes of the folk, the entire people, cannot conceivably be changed by a *coup d'état*, still less by a *coup de tête*. Society evolves, it moves not in leaps but in steps, and men can be outwardly enfranchised only in so far as they are inwardly free: 'the strength of the old order lies not so much in political power as in the fact that it is generally approved. We must influence men so that this approval may cease.' He was not a mere progressive, he declared. He was not looking for the new society to come from Western parliamentary democracy, but he didn't expect it to come from terrorism either. 'He who is unwilling that civilisation should be founded on the lash should not endeavour to secure liberty through the instrumentality of the guillotine.'[11]

There is a prophetic ring about his reflection that 'I think there is a certain basis of truth in the fear which the Russian Government is beginning to have of Communism: Communism is Russian autocracy turned upside down.' But it is not so much this kind of insight that brings us close to Herzen as his recognition that there are problems for which we will never find solutions, questions to which there are no answers. In his memoirs he writes:

> I was unhappy and perplexed when these thoughts began to haunt me. I tried by every means to run away from them. Like a lost traveller, like a beggar, I knocked at every door, stopped every one I met and asked my way. But every meeting and every event led to the same result—to humility in the face of the truth, to meek acceptance of it.

This discovery did not lead him, as it leads so many, to resignation and inactivity. He did not believe that because no road leads to Utopia, no road leads anywhere. From his earliest youth (he wrote to Mazzini), he had been waging a guerrilla war against every oppressive power in the name of the absolute independence of the individual. He would carry on this partisan struggle, he affirmed. He would be a genuine Cossack, acting on his own initiative. 'I am indeed attached to the great revolutionary army, but I will not enrol myself in its regular cadres until their character has been completely transformed.' For, he explained, he put his trust in people rather than in institutions, and he considered that simply to spread enlightenment is, in the long run, more important and more truly revolutionary. Herzen did not win his partisan engagement, but people and institutions being what they are, it is an engagement which can never be broken off completely.

Economics

Peter Kropotkin
(1842-1921)

Q UESTIONING PEOPLE about their childhood recollections, I am always struck by how often they remember lying on the hearthrug at their grandparents' house, turning over the pages of some big illustrated volume brought out for the occasion to keep the children amused. In my generation people remember yearly bound volumes of *Chums* or *Little Folks* from the turn of the century or popular illustrated histories of the first world war. Later generations recall books like the *Pip, Squeak and Wilfred Annual* for 1932.

At my grandfather's house in Essex it was a volume of *Titbits* from early in the century, its yellowing newsprint pages full of steel-engravings, a lost art of cheaply reproducing photographs and any other kind of illustration in those days. This was my first encounter with my economic influence, Peter Kropotkin. His article was about the building of the Trans-Siberian Railway, and was doubtless a digest of an account he had written for one of the geographical journals. Kropotkin was another of those extraordinary nineteenth-century Russians whose ideas seem on a global scale to fit the issues of the twenty-first century, as our own century has been wasted in an intoxication with profligate capitalist over-production on one hand, or authoritarian Marxist bureaucracy on the other.

I met him again when I was 14 in 1939 when *Mutual Aid* came out as a sixpenny Penguin. It argued that in any species cooperation succeeded and competition killed. It is an antidote both to managerialism and the worship of market forces. Then I bought a copy of the reprint published in the first world war of Nelson's 1912 revised and enlarged edition of *Fields, Factories and Workshops*. Kropotkin had argued that 'political economy, as it gradually emerges from its semi-scientific stage' tends to become a science devoted to the study of human needs 'and of the means of satisfying them with the least possible waste of energy'. And he claimed that 'The main subject of social economy—that is, the *economy of energy required for the satisfaction of human needs*—is consequently the last subject which one expects to find treated in a concrete form in economical treatises.'

And the publishers' note to that 1918 edition explained that the book 'pleads for a new economy in the energies used in supplying the needs of human life, since these needs are increasing and the energies are not inexhaustible'. Just ask yourself how long it has taken this simple proposition to enter the general consciousness—and it certainly hasn't yet—and you will see why I have ever since seen Kropotkin as my most valued economic influence. I have been connected with Freedom Press, the anarchist publishing house of which he was a founder in 1886, for forty years; I have edited two of his books for modern publication, and I consequently know as much about his limitations as about his strengths. For anyone who thinks seriously about an alternative economy, he is an immensely valuable precursor.

Kropotkin's *Memoirs of a Revolutionist* is another great masterpiece of Russian autobiography. The first part is one of those classic descriptions of an aristocratic childhood, told with exquisite clarity and perception. The second is a unique account of life in the Tsar's Corps of Pages, as absorbing for Kropotkin's educational reflections as it is for its glimpses of life at court in the early years of Alexander II, in whom such hopes had been placed after the emancipation of the serfs. A military career seemed inevitable, and with a privileged choice of regiments open to members of the Corps, he opted instead to serve with the Amur Cossacks in Siberia. This was thought to be an eccentric or bizarre decision. 'Are you not afraid to go so far?' the emperor asked him. 'No, I want to work. There must be so much to do in Siberia to apply the great reforms which are going to be made.' Then, Kropotkin continues, 'He looked straight at me; he became pensive; at last he said, "Well, go; one can be useful everywhere" and his face took on such an expression of fatigue, such a character of complete surrender, that I thought at once, "He is a used-up man; he is going to give it all up." '

Then his book opens out into a travel narrative, an account of his journeys in Siberia and in the central Asian territories recently annexed for the Russian empire by Bakunin's cousin Muraviev-Amurski. Few writers have conveyed so well that sense of inhabiting not a country but a continent, and it was his work there that gained him his reputation as a geographer. His theory of the orography of the Asian land-mass—the structure of its mountain systems—is the basis of the modern physical geography of Asia, and Kropotkin's hopes that his work would be of practical use in the development of the resources of the region have been fulfilled, though not in the ways he hoped. The geologist M.A. Novomeysky writes that Kropotkin's 700-page *Report on the Olekminsk-Vitimsk Expedition* was his 'desk-book' in that part of Siberia. 'I was inseparable from it in the days when I lived on the mining site, for in it I found much of the information that I needed in my work.'[1]

Kropotkin himself has a memorable passage on the sheer pleasure to be gained from scientific discovery:

There are not many joys in human life equal to the joy of the sudden birth of a generalisation, illuminating the mind after a long period of patient research. What has seemed for years so chaotic, so contradictory and so problematic, takes at once its proper position within an harmonious whole. Out of the wild confusion of facts and from behind the fog of guesses— contradicted almost as soon as they are born—a stately picture makes its appearance... He who has once in his life experienced this joy of scientific creation will never forget it; he will be longing to renew it; and he cannot but feel with pain that this sort of happiness is the lot of so few of us, while so many could also live through it—on a small or on a grand scale—if scientific methods and leisure were not limited to a handful of men.'[2]

It was in Siberia too, that Kropotkin extended his political education. The exiled poet Mikhailov introduced him to the works of Proudhon, and the brutal suppression of an attempted escape by Polish exiles led Kropotkin and his brother Alexander to resign their commissions and return to St Petersburg. The next part of his book describes his geographical work there, his expedition to Finland and his first visit to Western Europe, making contact with the socialist and anarchist movements. Once again his discovery of his political position was accompanied by a scientific discovery. He advanced what was then a completely heretical hypothesis that instead of floating icefields, there had been a glacial period in which much of Europe from the British Isles to most of Russia had been covered by a layer of glaciers in motion— a hypothesis which is now repeated in every textbook of geology and physical geography.

On his return from the West, he became a member of the Chaikovsky Circle, the most influential of the Russian populist groups of the 1870s, while continuing his geographical work. There is, as Paul Goodman remarked, 'a pathetic hilarity in the story that, whereas other agitators could get out of town and escape the police, he had to stay and explain to the Geological Society his thesis on the Ice Cap'[3]. There was of course nothing hilarious about it for Kropotkin, conscious as he entered the Peter-Paul fortress that it was here that the Decembrists were hanged and here that Bakunin had rotted. His book goes on to describe the captivity which permanently damaged his health, and his dramatic escape from the military hospital. The final section follows his arrival in Britain, his life in Western Europe as an anarchist propagandist and scientific journalist, his imprisonment in France, his assessment of some of the remarkable personalities of the anarchist movement, and his founding, with Charlotte Wilson, of the anarchist newspaper *Freedom*, which exists to this day. No reader will forget his chilling account of the assassination of Alexander II. For his public defence of the regicides he was expelled from Switzerland.

Kropotkin was in his mid-fifties when the *Memoirs* were written and most readers of that book will wonder about his subsequent life. When he finally settled in England with his wife and daughter, they lived very simply in small houses in Harrow, Bromley and finally Brighton. Kropotkin lost all his property when he escaped from Russia, and unlike other famous refugees, he never attempted to recover any, earning his living from his books, his contributions to scientific journals and to *The Nineteenth Century* where several of his books were serialised. In the early years of his English life he spoke at innumerable public meetings, on anarchism, or the prison system or the situation in Russia, and at trade union demonstrations like the Durham Miners' Gala or in support of minorities like the immigrant Jews in Whitechapel. All the while he was contributing to the anarchist press in English, French and Russian.

It was very useful for the anarchist movement to have this respected figure as a spokesman or intermediary, but his very eminence, both within the anarchist world and in society at large, led to his becoming for the anarchists a kind of oracle whose opinions were always right. The issue came to a head with his support of the Allied cause in the First World War, in opposition to the anti-nationalism and anti-militarist tradition not only of the anarchists but of the whole socialist movement. With a few exceptions, the majority of anarchists rejected his lead. For the first time in over forty years the official Russian press was open to Kropotkin, when his letter appeared in *Russkiia Vedomosti*, calling for Russians of every political view to join forces against German aggression. 'The old fool must have completely lost his mind' wrote Stalin to Lenin, and the opening pages of Solzhenitsyn's *August 1914* evoke the confusion that this political about-turn brought to ordinary obscure sympathisers inside Russia. Varya is dismayed to find Sanya caught up in the general war fever: 'Had he, her faithful mentor of old, taken leave of his senses too? She was not desperate to give him back the clarity of thought and firmness of will which he had once given her, to snatch him out of the whirlpool... The decades of 'civic' literature, the ideals of the intelligentsia, the students' devotion to the common people—was all this to be abandoned and cast aside in a single moment? Could they simply forget it all...?'[4]

Kropotkin did forget it all, and, wheeled around Brighton in a bath chair after two chest operations, was more isolated from those who shared his general outlook than ever before in his life. With the February Revolution and the abdication of the Tsar, Peter and Sophie Kropotkin (at the ages of 74 and 60) began packing for their return. He presented his desk, which had formerly belonged to Richard Cobden, to the Brighton Trades and Labour Club (which sixty years later gave it to the National Labour Museum) and set off via Aberdeen and Bergen, arriving at the Finland Station in Petrograd on 30 May 1917, where sixty thousand people, including Alexander Kerensky as head of the provisional government, were there to greet him. The anarchists, for the most part, were absent.

Even when faced with the realities of revolutionary Russia, Kropotkin went on advocating the continuance of the war. He was offered, and declined, a place in the provisional government, and was as surprised as anyone else by the success of the Bolshevik coup in October 1917. He settled at Dimitrov, forty miles from Moscow, and gradually re-established contact with the anarchists, with the guerrilla activists from the Ukraine like Makhno and Volin, and the deportees from the United States. In conditions of great hardship like those of most other Russians at the time, he worked on his book *Ethics*, published in an incomplete form after his death.

In 1920, with the visit of the British Labour Delegation, he entrusted to Margaret Bondfield his *Message to the workers of the West* and in the same year the Bolshevik government put a railway coach at the disposal of the English labour politician George Lansbury, in his capacity as editor of the *Daily Herald*. He brought with him an American journalist, Griffin Barry, and in the capacity of translators, three famous Russo-American anarchists, Emma Goldman, Alexander Berkman and Alexander Schapiro, who had been deported from the United States. Their conversations are described in Berkman's book *The Bolshevik Myth*, in Emma Goldman's *My Disillusionment in Russia* and in her autobiography *Living My Life*.[5]

Kropotkin's own letters to Lenin, dating from this period, are full of interest. In the first he intervened on behalf of the postal workers of Dimitrov, drawing attention to their situation, 'scurrying from office to office to secure permission to buy a cheap kerosene lamp'. This letter ends: 'One thing is certain. Even if a party dictatorship were the proper means to strike a blow against the capitalist system (which I strongly doubt), it is positively harmful for the building of a new socialist system. What is needed is local construction by local forces. Yet this is absent. It exists nowhere. Instead, wherever one turns there are people who have never known any real life committing the most flagrant errors, errors paid for in thousands of lives and in the devastating of whole regions.' Needless to say he received no reply, but, conscious of the fact that, whatever his own errors, he was regarded as an elder statesman of the revolution, Kropotkin wrote again to Lenin on 21 December 1920, six weeks before his death, to protest against the Bolshevik practice of taking hostages:

I have read in today's *Pravda* an official communiqué from the Council of People's Commissars, according to which it has been decided to keep as hostages several officers of Wrangel's army. I cannot believe that there is no single man about you to tell you that such decisions recall the darkest Middle Ages, the period of the Crusades. Vladimir Illich, your concrete actions are completely unworthy of the ideas you pretend to hold.

Is it possible that you do not know what a hostage really is— a man imprisoned not because of a crime he has committed, but only because it suits his enemies to exercise blackmail on his companions? These men must feel very much like men who have been condemned to death, and whose inhuman executioners announce every day at noon that the execution has been postponed until the next day. If you admit such methods, one can foresee that one day you will use torture, as was done in the Middle Ages.

I hope you will not answer me that Power is for political men a professional duty, and that any attack against that power must be considered as a threat against which one must guard oneself at any price...

How can you, Vladimir Illich, you who want to be the apostle of new truths and the builder of a new State, give your consent to the use of such repulsive conduct, of such unacceptable methods? Such a measure is tantamount to confessing publicly that you adhere to the ideas of yesterday. But perhaps, with the seizure of hostages, you did not try to save your work, but merely your own life? Are you so blinded, so much a prisoner of your authoritarian ideas, that you do not realise that, being at the head of European Communism, you have no right to soil the ideas which you defend by shameful methods, methods which are not only the proof of a monstrous error, but also of an unjustifiable fear for your own life? What future lies in store for Communism when one of its most important defenders tramples in this way on every honest feeling?[6]

Kropotkin died on 8 February 1921. The story is always told of how the imprisoned anarchists were released for one day to attend the funeral. In the same year Nestor Makhno's peasant armies were finally defeated in the Ukraine and the revolt of the Kronstadt Soviet was brutally suppressed by Trotsky. The black flag of the Russian anarchists was not seen again until the revolts in the labour camps after Stalin's death in 1953, and not, in Moscow, until the May Day demonstrations of 1990 when they were to be seen not only in Red Square, but outside Kropotkin's birthplace in the Shtatny Pereulok, long renamed Kropotkinski Pereulok.

More of Kropotkin's works are available in English today than at any time in the past, and none is more relevant to current discussion of our economic future than *Fields, Factories and Workshops*. One of its most persuasive advocates was Lewis Mumford who observed that

Almost half a century in advance of contemporary economic and technical opinion, he had grasped the fact that the flexibility and adaptability of electric communication and electric power, along with the possibilities of intensive biodynamic farming, had laid the foundations for a more decentralised urban development in small units, responsive to direct human contact, and enjoying both urban and rural advantages...[7]

His book made four major points. The first was that there is a trend for manufacturing industry to decentralise throughout the world, and that production for a local market is a rational and desirable tendency. The second was that this implies that each region of the globe must feed itself, and that intensive farming could meet the basic needs of a country like Britain. The third was that the dispersal of industry on a small scale and in combination with agriculture is also both feasible and desirable, and the fourth is that we need an education, and a habit of mind, that combines manual and intellectual work.

The combination of topics is unusual, and is explained by the framework of Kropotkin's thought. He was an anarchist, an advocate of society without government. He wanted the revolutionary overthrow of both capitalism and the state, and he envisaged production, distribution and social organisation in the hands of federated networks of autonomous communes. *The Conquest of Bread* is his manual for a revolutionary society, *Mutual Aid* is his treatise on social organisation, *Fields, Factories and Workshops* had several important functions in his system of ideas: firstly, to combat the view that there is any *technical* reason for the scale of industrial and agricultural organisation in modern society to grow larger and larger (which is a standard objection to anarchist and decentralist ideas); secondly—as a matter of revolutionary strategy—to cope with the problem posed by dependence on imported food which implies that a nation in revolt can be starved into submission; thirdly to advocate the kind of dispersed production for local consumption which is appropriate to the kind of society he wanted; and finally, to deny that the dehumanisation of labour is the price we must pay for a modern industrial society. His book is really a thesis (to adopt a phrase from Professor Stephen Marglin) on the *economic consequences of the humanisation of work.*

Writing at the time when Britain was still regarded as 'the workshop of the world', and when it was assumed by economists of both right and left that huge centralised factories were the industrial norm for the future, Kropotkin was arguing that

> The scattering of industries over the country—so as to bring the factory amidst the fields, to make agriculture derive all those profits which it always finds in being combined with industry and to produce a combination of industrial with agricultural work—is surely the next step to be taken... This step is imposed by the necessity for each healthy man and woman to spend a part of their lives in manual work in the free air; and it will be rendered the more necessary when the great social movements, which have now become unavoidable, come to disturb the present international trade, and compel each nation to revert to her own resources for her own maintenance.[8]

Prophecies seldom come true in the way that the prophets envisaged. People laughed at his view that Britain could be agriculturally self-sufficient. By the 1980s we had a crisis of over-production, reached by means which were not those he envisaged. They laughed at the emphasis he gave to the small workshop and its productive capacity. By the 1980s there were vast empty factories in all the old industrial centres of Europe and America. Let's not laugh at his final message. In December 1919, at the very end of his life, in the midst of the civil war that followed the Russian Revolution, Kropotkin wrote:

> Today, however, after the cruel lesson of the last war, it should be clear to every serious person and above all to every worker, that such wars, and even crueller ones still, *are inevitable so long as certain countries consider themselves destined to enrich themselves by the production of finished goods and divide the backward countries up among themselves, so that these countries provide the raw materials while they accumulate*

wealth themselves on the basis of the labour of others.

More than that. We have the right to assert that the reconstruction of society on a socialist basis will be impossible so long as manufacturing industry and, in consequence, the prosperity of the workers in the factories, depend as they do today on the exploitation of the peasants of their own or other countries.

We should not forget that at the moment is is not only the capitalists who exploit the labour of others and who are 'imperialists'. They are not the only ones who aspire to conquer cheap manpower to obtain raw materials in Europe, Asia, Africa and elsewhere. As the workers are beginning to take part in political power, the contagion of colonial imperialism is infecting them too... It is clear that in these conditions one may still predict a series of wars for the civilised countries—wars even more bloody and even more savage— if these countries do not bring about among themselves a social revolution, and do not reconstruct their lives on a new and more social basis. All Europe and the United States, with the exception of the exploiting minority, feels this necessity.

But it is impossible to achieve such a revolution by means of dictatorship and state power. Without a widespread reconstruction coming from below—put into practice by the workers and peasants themselves—the social revolution is condemned to bankruptcy. The Russian Revolution has confirmed this again, and we must hope that this lesson will be understood; that everywhere in Europe and America serious efforts will be made to create within the working class—peasants, workers and intellectuals—the personnel of a future revolution which will not obey orders from above but will be capable of elaborating for itself the free forms of the whole new economic life.[9]

In the light of events in the Soviet Union in the 1980s and 1990s, I am all the more inclined to listen to the views he expressed at its beginning:

> Imperial Russia is dead and will never be revived. All the attempts to bring together the constituent parts of the Russian Empire, such as Finland, the Baltic province, Ukraine, Georgia, Armenia, Siberia and others under a central authority are doomed to certain failure. The future of what was the Russian Empire is directed towards a federation of independent units.[10]

I find Kropotkin a very astute guide to the kind of economy, nationally or globally, that you and I actually want.

4

Society

Martin Buber
(1878-1965)

E VERY ONE OF MY INFLUENCES has had views to express about the
nature of human society. The reason why I found Martin
Buber to be the best explainer of everything I believe about
social organisation was precisely because he did it more simply
than anyone else. I came across Buber only because he was
frequently quoted by Herbert Read in articles in the anarchist
newspaper *Freedom*. Read was a director of the publishers
Routledge and in 1949 produced an English translation of Buber's
book *Paths in Utopia*. This was a re-assertion of the anarchist
tradition in socialist thought, ridiculed for decades both before
and after its publication by two kinds of state worship, that of
the Fabians and that of the Marxists.

Thereafter I watched Buber's sociological thought, and was won
over by his lecture on 'Society and the State' which crystallised a
range of ideas that, paradoxically, earned him only hostility. In
the 1950s my friend the architect Gabriel Epstein, whose parents
chanced to live in the same street in Jerusalem as Buber, confirmed

that the then Labour Party ruling elite in Israel saw him as a saboteur, not as a support. Thirty years later, a veteran *kibbutznik* told me that in his opinion Buber was 'just an old phoney', and, sure enough, when Buber died in 1965, The Guardian reported how 'In Palestine his idea of bi-nationalism caused him to be ostracised by the orthodox as "an enemy of the people" '.[1]

A philosopher who manages to antagonise everyone, yet who was himself a model of gentle benevolence, must have something important to say, I reflected, and I don't think I was wrong. His reputation was as a theologian, though I can remember him declaring to a puzzled clergyman on a BBC television programme that 'I must confess that I don't like religion very much', and parrying the suggestion that he was a mystic with the reply that he was in fact a rationalist, and the affirmation that rationalism was 'the only one of my world views that I have allowed to expand into an ism.'[2]

The only time I ever saw him was in 1956 at King's College in the Strand, where, lecturing on 'That which is common', he related his philosophy of dialogue, set out in his book *I and Thou*, with his views on community and society. He took as his text an account of Aldous Huxley's experiments with the drug mescalin, which became, in Buber's slow and emphatic English, a parable of what he saw as the disjointed society of western individualism. Huxley, in his escape from the 'painful earthly world' under the influence of the drug, found that his lips, the palms of his hands, and his genitals (the organs of communication with others, interpolated Buber) became cold, and he avoided the eyes of those who were present. For, said Buber, to look into the eyes of others would be to recognise that which is common. And after this flight from the self and from the ordinary environment, Huxley 'met them with a deep mistrust'. Huxley regarded his mescalin intoxication as a mystical experience, but, declared Buber, those whom we call mystics, like those we call creative artists, do not seek to escape from the human situation. 'They do not want to leave the authentic

William Godwin

Mary Wollstonecraft *portrait by John Opie*

Alexander Herzen

Peter Kropotkin

Martin Buber
photo: The Mansell collection

Bas-relief of William Richard Lethaby as
Master of the Art workers' Guild, 1911

Walter Segal congratulating a self-builder
photo by Phil Sayer

Patrick Geddes in Indore, Madhya Pradesh, India, 1911

Paul Goodman

world of speech in which a response is demanded. They cling to the common world until they are torn from it.'[3]

'My innermost heart,' he confessed, 'loves the world more than it loves the spirit,' and he embarrassed his chairman by leaping up the steps of the steep lecture theatre to question his questioners in order to discern what they really wanted to know.

For Buber held, as Herbert Read put it, 'that the communication of any truth, of any 'lesson', depends on the existence of a condition of mutuality between the teacher and the pupil—all effective communication is a dialogue...'[4] Buber has a different significance for different readers. For me he is a social philosopher, a sociologist in fact, who had grasped many decades ago the nature of the crisis of both capitalism and socialism. 'The era of advanced Capitalism,' he wrote, 'has broken down the structure of society. The society which preceded it was composed of different societies; it was complex and pluralistic in structure. This is what gave it its peculiar social vitality and enabled it to resist the totalitarian tendencies inherent in the pre-revolutionary centralistic State.' But socialism too, had fallen victim to state-worship, and 'if socialism is to emerge from the blind-alley into which it has strayed, among other things the catchword 'Utopian' must be cracked open and examined for its true content.'[5]

He wasn't an anarchist. He was an advocate of what he called socialist pluralism. But socialists have not yet caught up with him, neither in the west nor the east.

Buber was born in Vienna, a child of the Jewish enlightenment and emancipation, but when his parents divorced, went to live with his grandfather at Lemberg in Galicia. There he 'enjoyed his all-too-brief and trembling years of piety' and 'ceased in his formal obedience to Jewish law,'[6] but also discovered the pietistic sect, the Hasidim. As a student of philosophy in Vienna in the 1890s he encountered both the anarchist poet and propagandist Gustav Landauer and the Zionist movement. He was Landauer's collaborator, and after Laundauer's murder in the massacres following the

Munich 'council republic' in the wake of the first world war, his executor. Buber's relations with Zionism were stormy. For him it had nothing to do with hopes for a Jewish state: 'Although for many Zionism became the cloak of pride, the instrument of masking their alienation and lack of roots in European soil, it was for Buber the means of renewing roots, the ultimate device of re-establishing, not sundering contact, with the European tradition,'[7] as well as with the ideology of co-operative settlements propagated by secular, socialist pioneers like Aaron David Gordon.[8]

In the cataclysm that befell Germany, Buber left in 1938 and was appointed professor of social philosophy at the Hebrew University at Jerusalem. There he was more isolated, ideologically, than at any time in his life. 'During the strife that accompanied the prelude and consummation of the State of Israel, Buber assumed a position (the natural consequence of his spiritual Zionism) which alienated vast elements of the Israeli community. Arguing with Judah Magnes, Ernst Simon, and others, that the only solution to the Jewish problem was a bi-national state in which the Arabs and Jews should jointly participate and share, he aroused great bitterness and resentment.'[9]

In 1951 Buber was criticised for accepting the Goethe Prize of the University of Hamburg. Was he not, it was asked, in too much haste to forgive? His reply was to accept another German prize and in doing so, to say these words:

About a decade ago a considerable number of Germans—there must have been many thousands of them—under the indirect command of the German government and the direct command of its representatives, killed millions of my people in a systematically prepared and executed procedure whose organised cruelty cannot be compared with any previous historical event. I, who am one of those who remained alive, have only in a formal sense a common humanity with those who took part in this action. They have so radically removed themselves from the human sphere, so transposed themselves into a sphere of monstrous inhumanity inaccessible to my conception, that not even hatred, much less an overcoming hatred, was able to arise in me. And what am I that I could here presume to forgive!

When I think of the German people of the days of Auschwitz and Treblinka, I behold, first of all, the great many who knew that the monstrous event was taking place and did not oppose it. But my heart, which is acquainted with the weakness of men, refuses to condemn my neighbour for not prevailing upon himself to become a martyr. Next there emerges before me the mass of those who remained ignorant of what was withheld from the German public, and who did not try to discover what reality lay behind the rumours which were circulating. When I have these men in mind, I am gripped by the thought of the anxiety, likewise well known to me, of the human creature before a truth which he fears he cannot face. But finally there appears before me, from reliable reports, some who have become as familiar to me by sight, action and voice as if they were friends, those who refused to carry out the orders and suffered death or put themselves to death and those who learned what was taking place and opposed it and were put to death, or those who learned what was taking place and because they could do nothing to stop it killed themselves. I see these men very near before me in that especial intimacy which binds us at times to the dead and to them alone. Reverence and love for these Germans now fill my heart.[10]

Buber's book *Paths in Utopia*, completed in 1945, is a defence and restatement of that stream in socialist thought that was castigated by Marx and Engels as 'utopian', and was consequently ignored in the histories and university courses on political ideas.

It focusses in particular on the anarchist tradition represented by Proudhon, Kropotkin and Landauer. On the issue of *ends* and *means*, he explains that

> Kropotkin summed up the basic view of the ends in a single sentence: the fullest development of individuality 'will combine with the highest development of voluntary association in all its aspects, in all possible degrees and for all possible purposes; an association that is always changing, that bears in itself the elements of its own duration, that takes on the forms which best correspond at any given moment to the manifold strivings of all.' This is precisely what Proudhon had wanted in the maturity of his thought. It may be contended that the Marxist objective is not essentially different in constitution; but at this point a yawning chasm opens out before us which can only be bridged by that special form of Marxist utopics, a chasm between, on the one side, the transformation to be con-summated some time in the future—no one knows how long after the final victory of the Revolution—and, on the other, the road to the Revolution and beyond it, which road is characterised by a far-reaching centralisation that permits no individual features and no individual initiative. Uniformity as a means is to change miraculously into multiplicity as an end; compulsion into freedom. As against this the 'utopian' or non-Marxist socialist desires a means commensurate with his ends; he refuses to believe that in our reliance on the future 'leap' we have to have now the direct opposite of what we are striving for; he believes rather that we must create here and now the space *now* possible for the thing for which we are striving, so that it may come to fulfilment then; he does not believe in the post-revolutionary leap, but he does believe in revolutionary continuity.[11]

He was writing, of course, long before the 'forty wasted years' of the imposition of Marxist regimes on Eastern Europe. But when we examine capitalist society, Buber goes on, 'we see that it is a society inherently poor in structure, and growing poorer every day.' (By the structure of a society is to be understood its social content or community content: a society can be called structurally rich to the extent that it is built up of genuine societies: that is local communes and trade communes and their step by step association.) He compares Proudhon's views with those of Saint-Simon: 'Saint-Simon started from the reform of the State, Proudhon from the transformation of society. A genuine reconstruction of society can only begin with a radical alteration of the relationship between the social and political order. It can no longer be a matter of substituting one political regime for another, but of the emergence, in place of a political regime grafted upon society, of a regime expressive of society itself.'

Buber sees Kropotkin as amplifying Proudhon's thought in stating the simple antithesis between the principles of the struggle for existence and mutual help. He regards Kropotkin's earlier theory of the State as historically under-substantiated and sees as more useful the later view Kropotkin expressed in the French edition of 1913 of his *Modern Science and Anarchism*: 'All through the history of our civilisation, two contrary traditions, two trends, have faced one another; the Roman tradition and the national tradition; the imperial and the federal; the authoritarian and the libertarian.'

And he thinks that Gustav Landauer's step beyond Kropotkin consists in his insight into the State. For Landauer, 'The State is a condition, a certain relationship between human beings, a mode of human behaviour; we destroy it by contracting other relationships, by behaving differently.'

He examines the ideas of Marx, Engels, Lenin and Stalin, and shows how in their attitudes to co-operatives and workers' councils, as well as to the old Russian communal institutions, the *mir* and the *artel*, these are seen simply as tools in the political struggle. 'From the standpoint of Leninism,' said Stalin, 'the collective economies and the Soviets as well, are taken as a form of organisation, a weapon and nothing but a weapon.' One cannot in the nature of things, comments Buber, 'expect a little tree that has been turned into a club to put forth leaves'.

Everything about Buber's social philosophy draws him towards the co-operative movement, whether seen as consumer co-ops, producer co-ops or the idea of co-operative living. He begins with the obvious comment that

> for the most part the running of large co-operative institutions has become more and more like the running of capitalist ones, and the bureaucratic principle has completely ousted, over a wide field, the voluntary principle, once prized as the most precious and indispensable possession of the co-operative movement. This is especially clear in countries where consumer societies have in increasing measure worked together with the state and the municipalities, and Charles Gide was certainly not far wrong when he called to mind the fable of the wolf disguised as a shepherd and voiced the fear that, instead of making the State 'co-operative' we should only succeed in making the co-operative 'static'.[12]

Those of us who have spent a lifetime as members of ordinary retail co-operative societies in Britain would no doubt agree. We have seen the internal politics of the co-operative movement used as a stepping stone to office by politicians of the left. At the same time, we have watched (and this was a factor that Buber failed to observe) the local branch managers of retail co-operative societies lured away by a doubling of their wages by the capitalist chains of retail supermarkets.

But Buber moved on to examine the repeated attempts in the previous 150 years in both Europe and America to found co-operative settlements. He found that he had to apply the word *failure* not merely to those attempts, which after a short existence,

either disintegrated completely or took on what he saw as a
capitalist complexion, thus going over to the enemy camp. He
also applied a similar criticism to co-operative efforts which had
aimed at a wider style of co-operative living, but in isolation from
the rest of the world.

> For the real, the truly structural task of the new village
> communes begins with their *federation*, that is, their union
> under the same principle that operates in their internal
> structure. Even where, as with the Dukhobors in Canada, a
> sort of federation itself continues to be isolated and exerts no
> attractive and educative influence on society as a whole, with
> the result that the task never gets beyond its beginnings and,
> consequently there can be no talk of success in the socialist
> sense. It is remarkable that Kropotkin saw in these two
> elements—isolation of the settlements from one another and
> isolation from the rest of society—the effective causes of
> failure even as ordinarily understood.[13]

If the 'full co-operative' in which production and consumption
are united and industry is complemented by agriculture, is to
become the cell of a new society, it is necessary, Buber argues,
that 'there should emerge a network of settlements, territorially
based and federatively constructed, without dogmatic rigidity,
allowing the most diverse social forms to exist side by side, but
always aiming at the new organic whole.' He believed, in 1945,
that there was one effort 'which justifies our speaking of success
in the socialistic sense, and that is in the Jewish Village Commune
in its various forms, as found in Palestine.' He called the Kibbutz
movement a signal non-failure—he could not say a signal success,
because he was too aware of the setbacks and disappointments,
of the intrusion of politics, and of the 'lamentable fact that the all-
important attitude of neighbourly relationship has not been
adequately developed,' and of how much remained to be done.

There are two poles of socialism, Buber concluded, between which our choice lies, 'one we must designate—so long as *Russia* has not undergone an essential inner change—by the formidable name of Moscow. The other I would make bold to call *Jerusalem*.'

This polarity has not worn well. Nearly half a century later, there may well be essential inner changes in Moscow, though not in the direction Buber might have hoped. As for Jerusalem, few would see it as a beacon of socialism. It was as long ago as the 1920s that Buber warned the Zionist movement that if the Jews in Palestine did not live *with* the Arabs as well as *next* to them, they would find themselves living in emnity towards them.[14]

In 1950, as part of the celebration of the 25th anniversary of the Hebrew University of Jerusalem, Buber delivered his lecture on 'Society and the State'. He begins by citing the view of the sociologist Robert MacIver that 'to identify the social with the political is to be guilty of the grossest of all confusions, which completely bars any understanding of either society or the state'. Buber traces through sages from Plato to Bertrand Russell the confusion between the social principle and the political principle. The political principle is seen in power, authority and dominion, the social principle in families, groups, union, co-operative bodies and communities. It is the same distinction that Jayaprakash Narayan used to draw between *rajniti* (politics of the state) and *lokniti* (politics of the people). For Buber,

> The fact that every people feels itself threatened by the others gives the State its definite unifying power; it depends upon the instinct of self-preservation of society itself; the latent external crisis enables it when necessary to get the upper hand in internal crises.[15]

Administration in the sphere of the social principle, says Buber, is equivalent to government in that of the political principle. But,

All forms of government have this in common: each possesses more power than is required by the given conditions; in fact, this excess in the capacity for making dispositions is actually what we understand by political power. The measure of this excess, which cannot of course be computed precisely, represents the exact difference between Administration and Government. I call it the 'political surplus'. Its justification derives from the latent state of crisis between nations and within every nation... The political principle is always stronger in relation to the social principle than the given conditions require. The result is a continuous diminution in social spontaneity.[16]

Ever since I read these words I have found Buber's terminology far more valuable as an explanation of events in the real world and far more helpful than a dozen lectures on political theory or on sociology. They cut the rhetoric of politics down to size. Apply them for example to the politics of Britain in the 1980s. Governments used the populist language of 'rolling back the frontiers of the state' and of 'setting the people free', while at the same time pursuing policies of ruthless and pervasive central control, as in their war against the slightest independent policies of local authorities. Voluntary organisations too were manipulated into becoming the vehicles of government policy. The 'latent external crisis' in the form of the Cold War or the Falklands campaign was exploited 'when necessary to get the upper hand', and when the Cold War collapsed, the Gulf became a convenient successor.

If Buber's categories are observable in a relatively free society like Britain, they apply with dramatic force to the totalitarian regimes characteristic of the 20th century, which invariably sought to destroy all those social institutions they could not themselves dominate. The importance of the Catholic church in Poland or the Lutheran church in East Germany was not a matter of religious dogma, but in fact that they were among the few remaining alternative focii of power. Buber's 'continuous diminution in social spontaneity' is a feature of the Nazi period in Germany or the Bolshevik period in the Soviet Union, or indeed of Pinochet's Chile or Ceaucescu's Romania, that every survivor records.

Like Buber, I believe that the conflict between the social principle and the political principle is a permanent aspect of the human condition. He did us a service in excavating from Kropotkin's always optimistic writings the observation that the conflict between the authoritarian tradition and the libertarian tradition are as much part of the history of the future as of the past, and Landauer's view that this is not something that can be destroyed by a revolution.

If we want to weaken the state we must strengthen society, since the power of one is the measure of the weakness of the other. Buber's exploration of the paths to Utopia, far from confirming an acceptance of the way things are, confirms, as do several of my influences, that the fact that there is no route-map to utopia does not mean that there are no routes to more accessible destinations.

5

Architecture

William Richard Lethaby (1857-1931)
and
Walter Segal (1907-1985)

I DRIFTED INTO THE ARCHITECTURAL WORLD almost by accident and stayed on the drawing-board for twenty years. As my third job, when I was 16, I went to work for an elderly architect in Kensington. His practice, never large, had dwindled to patch-up repairs to bombed factories in Stepney, Poplar and Hackney.

He himself had been a pupil of the gothic revival architect John Loughborough Pearson, and had worked on the building of Truro cathedral, drawing full-size details for the masons on brown paper on a barn floor. In those days it was still universal to work on Saturday mornings, and he would urge me to make a creative use of Saturday afternoons by studying the ruins of Pearson's great London church, St John's, Red Lion Square, bombed in the previous year, to have the rare opportunity of *seeing* a gothic church in cross-section.

He had also been a student of, and then a colleague of, W.R. Lethaby in the early days of the Central School of Arts and Crafts, and although Lethaby had been dead for ten years, he talked about him as a living presence, and thrust into my hands Lethaby's little book *Architecture*, in the Home University Library series, which he told me, wrongly, would contain all I needed to know about architectural history. All this reverence flowed over me, and I had different uses for Saturday afternoons.

But in the end I read it, and everything else in the office library, which was entirely contained on the marble overmantel. There were the three well-worn blue volumes of Jaggard and Drury's *Building Construction*, Viollet-le-Duc's tome on *Rational Building*, Raymond Unwin's *Town Planning in Practice*, the Model By-laws and the London Building Acts and By-laws, Dorman Long's structural steel handbook, and a useful little book on sizes of timbers for floors and roofs. That was all, except for two other books by Lethaby which I absorbed with greater interest. One was *Philip Webb and his Work*, about the architect who built William Morris's Red House, but with very much more besides. The other was Lethaby's superb collection of essays, *Form in Civilisation*.

If I were an architect today I would yearn for the days when you could sail into the adventure of building with so slight a ballast, when the legislation was modest and comprehensible, and when the results were not plagued with leaks and condensation. For, as Lethaby remarked in his eulogy of the Victorian architect William Butterfield, 'In fact, notwithstanding all the names, there are only two modern styles of architecture: one in which the chimneys smoke, and the others where they do not.' I was lucky enough to discover Lethaby when I was very young, before I had learned that there were more sophisticated theories of architecture and its place in our lives.

The second of my big architectural influences was given to making the same kind of down-to-earth dictum as a mask for immense, lightly-worn erudition. Walter Segal was one of the only two of my chosen influences that I actually knew. Superficially the approaches to architecture of Lethaby and Segal were worlds apart. Lethaby was described by the author of *Architecture and*

Morality as 'a pleasingly eccentric product of the English Arts and Crafts movement overlaid with French rationalism,'[1] Segal was 'an architect who grew up in the centre of European Modernism', born in Berlin, the child of Romanian Jewish cousins, reared in Switzerland, accustomed to rootlessness and financial insecurity.

One thing they have in common is that, compared with the successful practitioners in either of their generations, each had a very small output. This is partly because both had a very scrupulous and old-fashioned conception of what it means to be a 'professional'. Both thought it meant giving a direct personal service to the client, and both turned down commissions that failed to meet their conceptions of what was worth doing. And even though they each built works full of technical interest for architects, both are more important for the way they formulated an attitude both to the art of building and to life. I was delighted to find this confirmed in John McKean's study of Segal. Discussing the influence of the socialist Arts and Crafts architects of the Morris tradition, he concludes that 'Segal responded to their empirical common-sense base, their social building goal and the writings of Lethaby. There are passages in Lethaby, for example on proportion and order, which recur almost word perfect in Segal.'[2] I wish both had been more influential.

Lethaby was the son of a Bible Christian picture-frame maker in Barnstaple, Devon, and escaped from a very prim and narrow background to become an architect (spending years as chief assistant to the redoubtable and inventive Norman Shaw), an agnostic (with an immense knowledge of the symbolism of ancient, early Christian and Muslim architecture), and a socialist (because 'to live on the labour of others is a form of cannibalism').

We admirers make pilgrimages to see the two or three buildings Lethaby left behind: Melsetter House on the island of Hoy in Orkney, or the beautiful little church at Brockhampton in Herefordshire, built in 1902, which has a *thatched* concrete roof. Lethaby thought of architecture as 'human skill and feeling shown in the great necessary activity of building,' but he believed that the very word had betrayed us: 'If we had no other words than *building* we might have been living in sound, watertight, well-lighted buildings.'

His legacy, all too unheeded, was in education. He tried, very hard, to change our attitudes and assumptions about it. He used to say that 'little can be proved: what matters is the quality of our assumptions.' His own were few and simple. He assumed that the most important thing in education, as in life, was art, and that 'the helplessness of modern art is the measure of the helplessness of the workers: there is justice in the universe.' He declared that 'those who believe in the condensed ignorance called Higher Education have succeeded with great difficulty in at last creating a dislike for that greatest of blessings, work.'

Lethaby's most striking, and all too short-lived achievement was in transforming art and design education. In the 1890s the infant London County Council set up a Technical Education Board, led by William Garnett and Sidney Webb. They appointed him first as its art inspector, and then enabled him to set up the Central School of Arts and Crafts and to make it the best school in Europe. (Among other things, modern typography was born there, as was the idea that the crafts should be taught by craftsmen, not by academics, an innovation that played havoc with the pay structure). At that time the Royal College of Art was regarded as the worst school of art in Europe, and Lethaby was appointed as the first professor of design there to try, against heavy opposition, to work the same kind of transformation again. When he finally retired, his students gave him a bicycle, appropriately, for he always used to claim that we should try to produce houses which were as efficient and economical as this humble master-piece of design.

There's a little contemporary vignette by Esther Wood of the early days of Lethaby's Central School of Arts and Crafts, which notes that 'Some curious varieties of personality and character may be seen in almost every room. Young and middle aged men, strong manual labourers, refined and scholarly-looking craftsmen, quiet earnest girls and smart little lads scarcely out of their fourth standard, are gathered together round the tables and desks or thinking out their designs plodding steadily on at some set task.'[3]

There is no school or college of art, craft or design in this country ninety years later to which such a description could apply. The educational ideal propagated by Lethaby and by William Morris and later craftsmen like Gimson and the Barnsleys in chair-making or Bernard Leach and Michael Cardew in pottery, has been abandoned quite deliberately by the education industry in which we all have an enormous vested interest, under the disguise of phrases like 'the balanced curriculum' or 'academic rigour'.

Within the world of architectural education, it almost seems that there was a conspiracy to bury Lethaby's particular wisdom. 'Writing of him in 1947, John Brandon-Jones expressed the frustration of a generation of architects and students who could have responded to Lethaby's initiatives if only they had known of them: "We seemed to be confined by stone walls and locked in by the solid oak doors of tradition. If we had but known it, Lethaby and his friends had left the key in the lock." '[4] John Brandon-Jones is a distinguished disciple of both my architectural influences, and forty years later was more explicit. 'My support for Walter, and my asking him to teach with me at the Architectural Association went very much in sympathy with my support of Webb and Lethaby. The common-sense of Lethaby and Walter Segal had very much in common... But it was most unfashionable. Furneaux Jordan the principal told me that if I didn't stop teaching students all that stuff from Webb and Lethaby, I'd destroy their faith in Modern architecture.'[5]

Lethaby was a modest and very independent man who declined offers, not only of the royal gold medal for architecture, but even of publication beyond his specialist studies of ancient buildings or for the building trades. But in honour of his 65th birthday, friends assembled a collection of his lectures and occasional articles under the title *Form in Civilisation: Collected papers on art and labour*, which gets reprinted every few decades.[6] It is a treasury of insight and wisdom, and I'm among those who remember whole passages by heart. Most of these essays were written during and after the first world war, and I have spent a lifetime pondering his remark in 1916 'For the earlier part of my life I was quieted by being told that ours was the richest country in the world, until I woke up to know that what I meant by riches was learning and beauty, and music and art, coffee and omelettes; perhaps in the coming days of poverty we may get more of these.'

No-one has yet thought it worthwhile to gather up Lethaby's fugitive papers of the 1920s written for modest publications of the Women's Rural Institutes, Dryad Handicrafts, the Salford Boy Scouts, and the Garden City Movement. When he was asked to write the chapter on 'The Town Itself', subtitled 'A Garden City *is* a town' in C.B. Purdom's collection *Town Theory and Practice*, he was obliged once again to declare his ultimate beliefs. 'The first thing you must do', he wrote, 'if you want to save civilisation, is to know what civilisation is.' He knew what it was. 'We have come to talk of music and drama and art and architecture as if they were technical words for remote abstractions or exceptional luxuries, but what is civilisation for, if it is not to produce poetry, music, beauty and courtesy? These things are nothing in themselves unless they have a use for life...'[7]

However self-effacing Lethaby was in his public life, it is evident that in private his conversation and reflections were a delight. His friends used to note down, and sometimes publish, the flow of aphorisms and witticisms that bubbled up in his casual talk. His sister-in-law, Grace Crosby, collected and recorded them, and his friend Alfred Powell called them 'just happy, intuitive reflections of his alert mind.'[8] Plenty of them stay in my mind:

> History is written by those who survive, philosophy by the well-to-do; those who go under have the experience.

> Governments dig themselves in: their true aim should be to become unnecessary.

We feel round the walls of our limitations, like a swallow in a barn.

It is a difficult world to be alive in! It makes one long for a sort of balcony to the world, so that one could go outside and get a breath of fresh air.

Lethaby's childhood background was in the narrow world of nonconformist piety among the skilled tradesmen of an English country town. Segal's was very different. In 1914, when he was seven, his parents moved to Ticino, the Italian-speaking canton of Switzerland. There, he tells us, Henri Oedenkoven, a Fleming from Antwerp, 'had founded a colony in which he and his confederates tried to find a new meaning of life'. This was Monte Verità, the Mountain of Truth, in the hills above Ascona. Other sources tell us that the co-founder was Karl Gräser, whose younger brother Gustav was met as he wandered through Germany with long hair, sandals and bare legs, by the writer Hermann Hesse, who immediately followed him down to Ticino, where Hesse was to spend most of his life.[9]

Monte Verità has its place in the footnotes of history simply because several of the writers, painters and revolutionaries who stayed there subsequently became world famous. Segal explains that 'The colonists abhorred private property, practised a rigid code of morality, strict vegetarianism and nudism. They rejected convention in marriage and dress, party politics and dogmas: they were tolerantly intolerant.'[10] Walter's father, Arthur Segal, was an expressionist painter, and 'we lived in abject poverty until one day a short and powerfully built man came, looked at the paintings and asked my father how much he needed to live on. My parents thought about 300frs. a month was the family's budget and the visitor undertook to be responsible for this; indeed he continued for nearly 30 years.' This fairy godfather was Bernhard Meyer, who in Walter's account was 'a peasant's son who became a millionaire and fanatical anarchist with a guilt complex about money. A friend of Kropotkin's during the latter's stay in Switzerland, he had founded an anarchist community at Rapperswyl on the Zurich Lake... and he supported and assisted countless people with a cause to fight for, though he never ceased to rebuke them for not joining the anarchist movement...'

I have frequently met people reared in self-consciously libertarian households who confess that they yearned to be like all the other kids, just as I have met plenty of that majority who have spent a lifetime escaping from their parents' automatic authoritarianism. Walter described how he decided early in life 'to be and stay average in the no-man's land between Bohème and Bourgeoisie'[11] He also explained the necessity of escaping from the milieu of Monte Verità into that of the village children in Ticino. 'So I had playmates in both camps which meant that I was affected by the lives of both the Bohemians and the ordinary philistines. And I have since found myself all the time moving from one camp to the other, never really able to adjust to one world only.' His conclusion was that 'To have spent childhood and adolescence in an environment of artists, architects, writers, life-reformers, thinkers and truthseekers, ideologues and mystics, charlatans and cranks, many of whom have left their mark upon our time—and unfortunately perhaps, continue to do so—was in a way a singular piece of good luck; but there were moments when I longed for ordinariness and went to seek it.'[12]

But there is another side to this. Peter Blundell Jones is quite right in saying that 'At Monte Verità Walter saw enough artistic self-indulgence to last a lifetime', but he is also right in perceiving that 'Walter was already steeped in far too rich and broad a culture and had become too much of a lone wolf ever to join any pack. He had to find his own way in everything, and confessed that he could never submit to authority.'[13] He was an outdoor child and knew very early in life that building was his business: 'So I gradually slid into an understanding of how buildings are put up, and it was clear to me by the age of fourteen that I was going to be an architect. This combination of designing and making was extremely important for me.' He was a student in the pioneering days of the Modern movement, but stayed independent of the ferment of ideas on design. 'I didn't really want to discuss with fellow students problems of architecture at all. I never joined that sort of thing. I just dismissed them. And when I was challenged on things, I would say: 'I don't know sufficient about these things. I've got first to know about *building* before I can have opinions on that kind of thing.'

His first building, in 1932, was a little wooden house, the Casa Piccola, for his father's patron Bernhard Meyer. I am one of the many people to whom he declared that his real good luck was when he picked up a book about the American tradition of 'Balloon-frame' house-carpentry in home and barn. He came to England in 1936, married Eva Bradt, who was a student at the Architectural Association, and worked on his own. As he used to say, he had always avoided being a wage-slave and saw no point in slaving to pay wages to others. Very few commissions came his way in the pre-war and post-war years, and he became a prolific and learned architectural journalist, collecting his studies of house-building in his book *Home and Environment*.[14] His buildings were technically inventive but otherwise unremarkable except for the endless trouble he had with the planning and building control system. He resisted the post-war giantism that swept over the architectural world, but had reached a professional crisis which he explained years later:

> Whenever a new project came along, there was this brief honeymoon with design, then the long drawn-out fight with the control apparatus. The client had to adjust himself to this. And then there was the final business of building, and there it was harder and harder. When you administer a client's resources you have a moral obligation to him. I built 30 houses in London before 1962 but it was becoming so difficult that it was really warfare—and I had become in consequence a much less amiable person than I am now. I was really quite

an unpleasant person to meet professionally.'[15]

His liberation began in 1962. Eva had died tragically young in 1950. Years later Segal and his second wife Moran Scott, with five children between them, decided to rebuild their house in Highgate and to put up a temporary bungalow at the bottom of the garden to live in meanwhile. The lightweight timber structure, with no foundations other than paving slabs, and using standard cladding materials and linings in market sizes (so that they could be re-used elsewhere), took two weeks to build and cost £800. Twenty-five years later it was still there, snug as ever. I slept in it one January with deep snow all around.

It aroused more interest than anything he had ever built, and led to a series of commissions up and down the country for permanent houses on the same principle, with Segal refining and improving the method every time. A carpenter, Fred Wade, followed him from house to house with the same reciprocal relationship he had established with the anarchist carpenter who built the Casa Piccola in 1932 or with Antonio Mesquida, the mason of the house he had built in Palma de Mallorca a few years later. Everywhere the clients found themselves able to do more and more of the building for themselves, to vary the plan and to make additions.

By the mid-1970s, Segal was yearning to find one local authority that would sponsor a built-it-yourself experiment of this kind for people on its housing waiting or transfer list. Eventually the London Borough of Lewisham decided by one vote to do so, on pockets of land too awkward or too sloping to fit its own programme. After two-and-a-half years of agonising delay—because the proposal did not fit the standard ways of financing, providing or controlling buildings—it happened.

The members of the Lewisham Self-Build Housing Association were lyrical about their achievement and the way it had changed their lives. Segal recalled his feelings when the first frame went up: 'I was immensely happy, like a child almost.' It wasn't just a vindication of his building method and its relevance in a country with a need for cheap, quick, yet durable housing, and with people in unsought idleness. It was a triumph for his belief that people could—if aided rather than pushed around—manage their own lives and shape their own environment. And instead of being dismayed at the 'countless small variations and innovations and additions' to the designs he had worked out with each individual family, he rejoiced that 'there is among the people that live in this country such a wealth of talent,' and he found it unbelievable that this creativity would continue to be denied outlets.[16]

When I last spoke to him, a few weeks before he died, he was bubbling with enthusiasm about a demonstration structure erected at the Centre for Alternative Technology in Wales, and about a building his stepson was putting up on his smallholding, with three big frames, put up like an American barn-raising, by emptying the local pub one weekend lunchtime. By the end of his life he was the most happy and contented architect any of us is likely to meet.

6

Planning

Patrick Geddes (1854-1932)
and
Paul Goodman (1911-1972)

F OR AS LONG AS I CAN REMEMBER, I have been absorbed by the
ways in which people use, manipulate and shape their
environment. I was thrilled as a child by Robert Flaherty's old film
Nanook of the North where, in the most inhospitable climate
imaginable, the Eskimo family met its building needs with ice,
bones and skins. Years later I read Flaherty's conclusion that 'These
people, with less resources than any other people on earth, are
the happiest people I have ever known.'

The world of shanty towns, seaside chalets and allotment
gardens has always meant more to me than the official
environment made by the people who controlled access to land
and resources and imposed an official plan on everyone else. I'm
sure that other people share this view, even though they fail to
draw appropriate conclusions from their experience. For example,
when the English describe the delights of Paris as a city, it isn't
Haussmann's imposition of geometry on the mediaeval city that
excites them, but the spaces in between. And when visitors go

to Brasilia, the planned capital city, they are always told that if
they want to sample Brasilian food, culture and music—all those
things that Lethaby insisted were the real riches of any society—
they have to drive out to the *Cidades Libres*, the squatter settlements
outside the official city, home of the building workers who
constructed it, but who could never afford to live there.

When I was a child, the opinion-formers were wild about
planning, by which they meant the impositions of centralised
government. Admirers of Mussolini explained that he made the
trains run on time and drained the Pontine Marshes. (He and
who else, you might ask?) Or they praised Hitler for building
Germany's *autobahnen*, the motorways that enabled the rich,
the party bosses and the army to get anywhere quickly. Or they
exalted over Stalin's Five Year Plans, which were going to enable
the Soviet Union to outstrip the capitalist powers in providing
for the needs of ordinary people.

The admiration for other people's dictators came home to roost.
Post-war governments believed implicitly in planning, and this
belief infected ordinary citizens, to reinforce the view that central
government knows best. You still meet people who put their faith
in a centralised transport policy and associate this with one political
party rather than its rivals. Every now and then it emerges, usually
in public enquiries on crucial planning issues, that no British
government ever had a transport policy (we learned this from the
Roskill Enquiry in the 1970s on the siting of a third London airport)
nor an energy policy (we learned this from the Layfield Enquiry
in the 1980s on the Sizewell proposal to build a nuclear power
station there). In both cases the official view won.

Planning as a governmental activity is firstly a sham, and secondly
a means by which the rich and powerful impose their control of
everyone's resources on the poor and powerless. But there have
always been people who saw it as something quite different.

I've had a friend for the last forty years, John Turner. His experience
in *barriadas*, *favelas* and *pueblos jovenes* in the exploding cities
of the poor countries of Latin America, made him able, among

other observers, to change the world's mind about the miles of self-built settlements in the continents that are described as the Third World.[1] He is as aware as anyone else of the patchy and partial way in which his message has been received.

What interests me is the way he came by a different way of seeing poor people's approach to planning. He explains that 'For some minor misdemeanour at the English public school I attended, a prefect made me read and précis a chapter of Lewis Mumford's *The Culture of Cities*. Mumford quoted his own teacher, Patrick Geddes, whose name stuck in my mind. Later, Geddes' work caused me to doubt the value of my professional schooling and, when I eventually escaped into the real world, his work also guided my deschooling and re-education.'[2]

I encountered Geddes too through the work of Lewis Mumford, in less obligatory circumstances, but if I meet a student who proposes to write a dissertation around the mounds of papers Geddes left behind, now gathered in heaps in the National Library of Scotland, and in Edinburgh and Strathclyde universities, I always warn them off. If I were wandering down the street I would probably cross the road to avoid being buttonholed by him and hectored for half an hour about what we should do with our inheritance. But other people have distilled the essence of his message better than he could.

Influences get passed on by accident, and it was our good fortune that as a 20-year-old student in New York in 1915, Mumford had the luck to come across two of the books that Geddes managed to complete, *City Development* and *Cities in Evolution*. He was thus introduced to a range of thinkers and their ideas who were way beyond the academic reading lists, like the anarchist geographers Elisée Réclus and Peter Kropotkin, and the garden city pioneer Ebenezer Howard. Geddes was the key influence in his subsequent work. They met in London in the 1920s, and Mumford later described how the old man not only perceived that here was the long-sought interpreter of his fragmentary thoughts, but also saw him as, and almost confused him with, the cherished son lost in the first world war: the poignancy of the situation was brought back to Mumford by the loss of his own son, named after Geddes, in the second.[3]

Geddes was born in Aberdeenshire and reared in Perth; though most of us associate him with Edinburgh, after his training as a marine biologist, he was never on good terms with the city authorities, nor with the university there. He failed to get any of the teaching jobs he applied for, and was finally made a professor of Botany at Dundee simply because a philanthropist endowed a chair for him.

He was the kind of prophet who leaves behind disciples like Mumford, but no coherent body of theory. But quite a lot of the language of planning comes from him. He invented the slogan Survey Before Plan, and he also coined the word *conurbation*, meaning the growing together of several urban settlements. He believed that the key to the understanding of any city and its rural hinterland was through the geographical concept of the Valley Section in which he linked characteristic traditional occupations with the terrain in which they occurred. Thus he thought that it added to our understanding of the way society worked if we conceived of urban equivalents to these rural occupations: from miner to engineer, woodman to builder, hunter to soldier, shepherd to weaver and so on. He also adapted the language of archaeology to define two contrasting phases of industrial civilisation as *paleotechnic* and *neotechnic*.

In the view of his most creative follower, Lewis Mumford, Geddes ignored the phase in human history that preceded both, 'the important period of preparation, when all the key inventions were either invented or foreshadowed'. To this 'dawn age of modern technics', Mumford gave the label *eotechnic*, and he explained, following Geddes, that 'speaking in terms of power and characteristic materials, the eotechnic phase is a water-and-wood complex, the neotechnic phase is an electricity-and-alloy complex.' The first half of Mumford's Geddesian book *Technics and Civilisation* is a history of European civilisation in terms of the social, political and cultural responses to these phases of technology.

These phases do not follow in any crude or mutually exclusive way: they co-exist, overlap and interpenetrate. If we look around the rooms in which I am writing and you are reading, we can see that the table and chairs are likely to be eotechnic, the stove paleotechnic and the television neotechnic, or produced by technologies which scarcely existed when either Geddes or Mumford was writing, but that the energy sources that produced them are a mixture of all three phases. But what of the *people* who produced them?[4]

Geddes was a philosopher of town and country planning who saw it not as a professional, but as a popular activity. He was the prophet of regionalism, of regional survey and regional reconstruction. But he believed that the only really useful planning was ordinary, practical, day-to-day activity, rather than campaigns to persuade governments to do things. He didn't believe in sitting around and playing politics. Paddy Kitchen, one of his biographers, describes his first move in Edinburgh:

> His first major step towards practical civic renewal was taken in 1886 when, as a university lecturer of thirty-two, he took his new wife, Anna, to live in the tenement slums of old Edinburgh in order to teach the impoverished community how to renew their environment. He persuaded neighbours to put colour washes on the walls of the old dank closes, to brighten the tenement facades with window boxes, and while he organised the installation of bathrooms he pointed out to the authorities the follies of demolition when it left the native citizens of a town with nowhere to go. At the same time he and a group of friends and businessmen bought up nearby properties and converted them into the first self-governing student hostel in Britain.[5]

When you consider the recurring phases of 'urban renewal' in British and American cities with their unspoken agenda of driving the poor out of town, you can see the importance of Geddes' activities a century ago. Yet another of the initiatives he set in motion is the Outlook tower at the western end of that wonderful sequence of streets in Edinburgh known as the Royal Mile. This is a tall, much-altered Burgher's house dating from the 17th century to which a previous owner had added a turret containing a camera obscura, that delicious optical toy, which was called Short's Observatory. Geddes, deeply involved at the time in slum improvements in the wynds and closes of the Old Town, instantly saw the potentialities of the building, and bought it in 1892, with borrowed money. Another of his biographers, Philip Mairet, after describing the breath-taking panorama of the city and the hills beyond, which the camera obscura provides, goes on to explain the 'sociological museum and laboratory' which Geddes created in the building:

> In the cupola that crowns the 'dark chamber' a mirror, rotated at will, projects the image of this scene through a lens upon a white table for the viewer below. With eyes rested by the low light of the interior and focussed one by one upon the changing aspects of height and hollow, light and shade, colour or gloom, the beholder moves round the circular table as the viewpoint is moved round the horizon, and is invariably captivated by the sheer beauty of the living picture...

> When Geddes took possession of the building he gradually furnished it throughout with the charts, diagrams, friezes and instruments of a world survey. The whole was arranged as an 'index museum' to the universe, seen from this point in Edinburgh. Thus the lower octagonal room upon which the camera was perched contained astronomical charts and apparatus demonstrating fundamental cosmic phenomena such as the orbit of the earth among the other heavenly bodies, and the apparent movement of the stars, shown by a hollow celestial globe which one could enter and view the whole

sphere of stars from within. The episcope—an instrument designed by Paul Réclus—presented an image in depth, by which one could 'see through' any chord of the terrestrial sphere to any point in Europe, Asia or America, or the Antipodes. And outside this room, on the parapet, a fixed telescope took the observer's eye to the horizon, aided by arrows incised in the stones, pointing to the features of the landscape, far and near.[6]

Mairet's account presents something of the pathos of Geddes' heroic endeavour. He wanted to combine direct involvement of every citizen and child in her or his own environment with an attempt to bring the whole of human knowledge into that citizen's range. The vehicle was a virtuoso use of visual aids, accumulated with endless ingenuity, and superseded a century later by video and television, where an army of skilled technicians can, between advertisements for soap powders or deodorants, provide the same synoptic overview of geography and history that this pioneer and his handful of disciples tried to achieve. For Philip Mairet's description goes on to explain that

Below this, in the Scotland Room the evolution of the Scottish nation was traced through to the opening future; a great floor map (oriented with the Outlook still in mind) provided a key to the geographical factors in social development. Like that of the Edinburgh Room, repeatedly re-arranged, the collection was designed to illustrate the main principles of the Geddes survey method. The floors lower down were occupied by surveys of Britain as a whole and the Empire, Europe and other continents, still in descending circles, and lastly the World Room containing two globes, one of relief and the other of vegetation. This was the general layout, constituting a kind of regional and world encyclopaedia, but the arrangement was intended also to facilitate studies from the standpoint of the social sciences, in accordance with their synthetic order as elaborated by Geddes. And here the aim was practical: there was abundant illustration, from the history of Edinburgh itself ('Go outside and verify with your eyes' Geddes would say) of the accumulated inheritance of good and burden of evils, which successive generations of citizens have to develop and to remedy. What is now well-known as 'regional survey' started from this elaborate demonstration. The Tower exhibited typical samples of social and civic maldevelopments side by side with creative plans of redevelopment, actual and possible.[7]

The Outlook tower was thus conceived as an educational device, a planning tool and a vehicle for citizen participation. Peter Green from Strathclyde University was another scholar who got buried in the mouldering piles of paper Geddes left behind, but managed to emerge in the 1970s with a new edition of Geddes' book *City Development*, which set out to be nothing more than a study of the future of parks and gardens in the small Scottish manufacturing town of Dunfermline. Green explained that 'Patrick Geddes wanted every town to have its Outlook Tower housing a civic exhibition, to promote a public awareness of what could be achieved by sensible civic planning and co-operative action. He anticipated by some fifty years the idea that the average citizen has something positive to contribute towards the improvement of his environment. Geddes was convinced that each generation has the right to inbuild their own aspirations into the fabric of their town. In order to achieve this a basis of civic understanding has to be created through education. Geddes canvassed schools, societies and associations and attempted to draw them into making surveys and plans of their locality; creating play-spaces, planting trees, and painting buildings. He seized on any vehicle to expose people to situations in which they had to make judgements.'[8]

The direct expression of ordinary citizens' aspirations in the reshaping of the town or city is the environmental message that comes from so many of Geddes' environmental perceptions. It was ignored both by public authorities and speculative developers in the rebuilding of British cities. But one of the ironies of his singularly unsuccessful life as an urban planner was that, having failed to be commissioned by the city fathers in Britain, he was hired to produce planning surveys for a range of municipal councils and local maharajahs in Indian cities, in the years between 1914 and 1922. These reports, like those he produced in British cities, could have been put away in cupboards and forgotten, but for the fact that their immense understanding of the needs of the poorest of citizens led to their re-discovery many decades later.

I have before me, for example, a reprint from 1965, produced by the Planning Commission of the government of Pakistan, reproducing Geddes' reports on 'Urban improvements: a strategy for urban works for Lahore and Dacca. The editors explain that 'The Lahore Report was discovered in its original printed form, however the Dacca Report has been found only in a typescript form,' and that 'of the many reports he wrote in India few have received very wide circulation, many have never been published, probably some have been destroyed and others must certainly still exist in the files of Municipal Councils waiting only for somebody with the patience and initiative to discover them.'[9]

Fortunately, the British planner Jacqueline Tyrwhitt, who had re-edited Geddes' book *Cities in Evolution* after the second world war,[10] had also produced a selection of his Indian planning reports in 1947 under the title *Patrick Geddes in India*, illustrated with a marvellous collection of photographs by Anthony Denney.[11] This book provided its author's ultimate challenge. For Geddes, with his endless schemes and diagrams, intended to contain the whole of human knowledge, was able to look at Indian cities from the standpoint of their humblest inhabitants. Many decades later, consultants from the rich world were employed at great expense to prepare great schemes for the redevelopment of the poor world's cities. Sometimes the plans were actually put into effect, adding to the burden of the poor majority of the inhabitants.

It was their aspirations that Geddes appreciated. He advocated the policy he described as 'conservative surgery': the minimum interference with existing dwellings and districts, so as to retain the pattern of the old bazaar town. He recognised that 'The craftsman and artist at their labour, the housewife at her daily tasks, the girl watering a tulsi-plant, the sweeper on his humble round, all and each are helping their town towards its development in health and wealth.' In other words he saw the importance of the informal, invisible economy. He saw the importance of small improvements 'with only moderate effort and expenditure', so that 'The woman returns from the repaired well with purer water and uninfected feet, and from small beginnings, begetting delight instead of disgust, a new interest in sanitation will arise.' Perhaps the most intuitive of his perceptions from those days, important for anyone, East or West, who believes that future urban populations can be *confined* to the city, was his declaration that, 'I have to remind all concerned, first that the essential need of a house and family is *room*, and secondly that the essential improvement of a house and family is *more room*.'[12]

It is no wonder that John Turner, our foremost advocate of *dweller control* as the first principle of housing, whether we are talking about Britain, the United States, Latin America or South-East Asia, draws sustenance from a chance remark by Geddes in 1912, 'For fulfilment there must be a resorption [the word he was looking for was re-absorption] of government into the body of the community. How? By cultivating the habit of direct action instead of waiting upon representative agencies.'[13]

This decentralist, anarchist approach permeates his thought. At the end of the first world war Geddes issued an ideological challenge to the centralist assumptions of all the politicians:

> The central government says, 'Homes for heroes? We are prepared to supply all these things from Whitehall; at any rate to supervise them; to our minds much the same thing.' But are they? Can they? With what results, what achievements? At present we have the provinces all bowing to Westminster,

whence they are granted doles; so the best people leave for London. They send their money to Westminster, which (after ample expenses have been deducted) is returned to some of them in the alluring form of a grant. But why not use this money themselves in the first place? Why not keep your money, your artists and your scientists, your orators and your planners—and do up your city yourselves?[14]

Here he was touching upon a key issue which is even more relevant today. We are conditioned to look at local government, and practically every other facet of society in Britain, from the top down. Geddes, like his anarchist friends, looked from the bottom up. The excuse for central government and for central revenue-gathering is to equalise the differences of income generated by different regions. But daily observation shows that, even with the most sophisticated systems of revenue-gathering, it doesn't happen. Poor districts, like poor people, stay poor. And the last thing that central government is willing to yield to regions, counties or districts, is the right to revenue-gathering. Centralised taxation is always justified by reference to its redistributive effect. Geddes and his successors invite us to examine just how redistributive it has actually been.

He can't really be placed politically. For example, he once wrote an article for the annual report of the Co-operative Wholesale Society with the title, paradoxical for many socialists, 'Co-operation *versus* Socialism'. His objections to socialism as an ideology, rather than as an ordinary habit of daily life, were, he said, because it too often meant dreaming dreams, but not actually getting anything done, and because it implied that 'until every thing and everybody is ready for the millenium, nothing can be got really ready at all.' Whereas, in his view, co-operation 'does the daily duties which lie nearest, refuses no bird in the hand today for the sake of two in the bush tomorrow, and thus not only lives and grows, but daily strengthens towards larger tasks; since, in fact, getting a bird into the hand today is the best practice for getting two out of the bush tomorrow.'[15]

Ideas poured out from Geddes in a stream of prophecies which both thrilled and exasperated his listeners. Something of their flavour is given in a tribute by our foremost urban geographer Peter Hall:

> From Réclus and Kropotkin, and beyond them from Proudhon, Geddes also took his position that society had to be reconstructed not by sweeping governmental measures like the abolition of private property, but through the efforts of millions of individuals; the 'neotechnic order' meant 'the creation, city by city, region by region, of a Eutopia'. After World War One he believed that the League of Nations should be a league of cities—and not of the capitals, which were centres of the war-machines, but of the great provincial cities which, regaining their former independence, would then voluntarily federate on a Swiss model. This idea prompted a characteristic outpouring, which demands extended quotation—though in Geddesian terms, it is a mere fragment. '... Federate homes into co-operative and helpful neighbour-hoods. Unite these grouped homes into renewed and socialized quarters—parishes, as they should be—and in time you have a better nation, a better world... Each region and city can learn to manage its own affairs—build its own houses, provide its own scientists, artists and teachers. These develop-ing regions are already in business together; can't they make friends and organize a federation as far as need be... May this not be the time prophesied by Isaiah?...' When his bemused questioner tried to get him to explain himself, he replied that a flower expressed itself by flowering, not by being labelled.[16]

Geddes was an influence people came across by chance: the way that Mumford or Turner or I discovered him. My other big planning influence wasn't a planner either. He was Paul Goodman, who saw himself as a poet and novelist, but who, with his brother

Percy, wrote the best of all accounts of the choices that face all of us who get involved in the future of the human environment.

I came across Paul Goodman's name because at the end of the war Freedom Press in London distributed half a dozen anarchist and pacifist journals from the United States. There was *Why?*, later *Resistance*, produced by a group of New Yorkers which included Paul. There was *Retort*, printed and edited by Holley Cantine and Dachine Rainer, and there was Dwight Macdonald's *Politics*. Later came *Liberation*.

His was an unmistakable voice because of a particular style of thinking which, in his words, 'aims at far-reaching social and cultural advantages by direct and rather dumb-bunny expedients'. In 1946, in his book *Art and Social Nature* he explained his point of view:

> A free society cannot be the substitution of a 'new order' for the old order; it is the extension of spheres of free action until they make up the most of social life... The libertarian is rather a millenarian than an utopian. He does not look forward to a future state of things which he tries to bring about by suspect means; but he draws now, so far as he can, on the natural force in him that is no different in kind from what it will be in a free society, except that there it will have more scope and will be immeasurably reinforced by mutual aid and fraternal conflict.[17]

I was in touch with him for years, simply over reprinting his articles from minority journals in one country in those of another. In 1960 he suddenly became a national figure through his book *Growing Up Absurd*. He handled this situation characteristically, modifying neither his casual and disreputable behaviour nor his radical anarchist message, though welcoming the end of his years of poverty and the instant readership for anything he cared to write. I only met him once, sitting on Roger Barnard's front lawn in London in 1967. After his death in 1972, interest in his views declined, though a mutual friend Taylor Stoehr edited several volumes of his essays, poems and stories.

Indeed, in a recent essay on 'Rereading Paul Goodman in the Nineties' Professor Stoehr points to his continuing relevance:

> Many of those ideas are now part of common knowledge and experience, as they were from the start part of common sense. They were never his creation or property—they were truths of human nature, traditional wisdom remembered at a moment of impasse, attitudes necessitated by our crisis. I am thinking for example of Goodman's anarchist call for decentralisation and local autonomy based in community life; his urging a more livable balance of urban and rural values; his reminder that technology properly belongs under the jurisdication of moral philosophy and not the R&D teams of the corporations or the Pentagon; his critique of the lockstep educational system and the art-killing mass media devoted to a wasteful, venal standard of living. Although we cannot say that such ideas have now won the day in any practical way, they are surely part of our truth, and Goodman one of our guides to making it practical.[18]

The book I value most in the whole Goodman output was the one that Paul and his architect brother Percival wrote during the war, *Communitas: Ways of Livelihood and Means of Life*. In wartime the drawing boards of architects and planners become bare. It is a time when all societies live on hope: that present sacrifices may bring future rewards, that guilt over past neglect may produce resolution for subsequent social justice. Dozens of books were written on both sides of the Atlantic on the ideas that should guide the post-war reconstruction of towns and cities. Most are totally forgotten. One remains relevant and exciting. The unemployed architect and the draft-dodging anarchist collaborated between 1942 and 1945 on *Communitas*, which was published by the University of Chicago in 1947.

The small edition soon went out of print and for years the book had a kind of underground, word-of-mouth existence, thanks to the advocacy of academics like David Riesman and writers like Lewis Mumford. They found it was the only modern contribution to the art of building cities which 'deals with the underlying values and purposes, political and moral, on which planning of any sort must be based'. It was reprinted as a paperback in 1960, with a new chapter on banning cars from cities. The Goodmans noted of the New York regional plan, as they might of the Greater London development plan, that 'the effect is to create blighted areas in the depopulated centre and to accelerate conurbations at the periphery. The highways, particularly, draw on the social wealth mainly for the benefit of the upper and middle class: for the poor can afford neither the houses nor the automobiles.'[19]

Their book is in two parts, first a critique of modern plans, followed by the brothers' own 'practical proposals'. They see a 'community plan' not as a layout of streets and houses, but as the external form of human activity, 'more like a choreography of society in motion and at rest, an arrangement for society to live out its habits and ideals and do its work, directing itself or being directed.' They examine in turn the three main types of plan which emerged in the preceding century, grouping them into green belt plans, industrial plans and integrated plans, and they ask what each expresses or presupposes about domestic life, psychology of work and leisure, education, political initiative, aesthetics, economic institutions, and practical realisation.

The Goodmans view green belt plans as emerging from the nineteenth-century reaction against the ugliness and squalor of the factory system. Moralists like Ruskin, Morris and Wilde wanted to scrap both the technology and the profit system to recreate pre-industrial values, while meliorists like Howard sought to make it possible for people to live decently 'with' industry. But 'whereas for Howard the protected homes were still near, and planned somewhat in conjunction with, the factories, the entities that are now called garden cities are physically isolated from their industry and planned quite independently.' As for garden city culture, 'the community spirit belongs, evidently, to those who stay at home. Just as the suburb belongs pre-eminently to the children, here the community belongs to the children and certain of the women. To the men and women who commute homeward, there is offered the golf course and other congenial surroundings in which to talk business.'

Le Corbusier's *Ville Radieuse* they characterise as a different kind of garden city: the centre is opened out to relieve congestion so that both homes and centre are green. 'It is a *Cité Jardin*: that is, the ratio of empty space is large, and there are fields for outdoor sports right at one's doorstep, if one had a doorstep.' It is 'conceived with theoretical severity and with the daring practicability possible only to one rejoicing in his time, the high capitalism of the captains of industry (so Le Corbusier calls them)'. But by the same token, the *Ville Radieuse* is 'the perfecting of the status quo of 1925, that as an ideal has already perished. The city was founded on the distinction of classes and the most striking expression of the distinction, just when the wealthy class was about to assume a protective camouflage. Those brains and eyes of society are called captains of industry, but their function is to study the market and exploit labour.'

The *Ville Radieuse* was a consumer city where 'in a sense, the city itself was the chief consumption product'. The Goodmans turn next to city plans centred on production. From the debates in the USSR before the second five year plan, four types of city plan emerged. The first three were the political-industrial concentration in Moscow, the 'left deviation' of the functionalists, and the plan of the 'disurbanists'. The first of these emerged as the 1935 plan for Moscow, 'made half of baroque dreams remembered from czarism and half of imitations of successful capitalist cities', in an attempt 'to evoke social solidarity and satisfaction through price and grandeur'.

As an example of a technological plan for an advanced economy, the brothers then consider Buckminster Fuller's Dymaxion scheme of 1929-32, based, so far as housing is concerned, on lightweight mass-produced shelters, 'free as a ship of public utilities, sewerage, water'—early versions of the self-sufficient house that some people build for themselves today. But Fuller's social thinking lagged behind his technical ingenuity.

Their final group of plans are those which sought to integrate city and country. They insist that we must distinguish between this union under conditions of scarcity and under conditions of surplus. 'In scarcity, it may be an economic solution fraught with drudgery worse than the worst technological scheme. But in sufficiency, it is the means of conserving and extending a way of life and of finding new values in the technical means of livelihood. In the course of history, the diversified farm, when successful, has always provided a real, though sometimes narrow, satisfaction of life to both sexes and all ages, just as the cities have been the places of politics, art, and social congregation. Any scheme that combines with urban sophistication the depth of rural self-sufficiency—that would *deserve* to be called a plan.'

First among the integrated plans comes Frank Lloyd Wright's Broadacres, with its density of one person per acre, denser here and sparser elsewhere, spread over the entire countryside. It is based on small farming and vaguely decentralised industry, a formula more tightly argued by Ralph Borsodi, who for years had insisted that by cutting out the costs of transportation, marketing, and tribes of middlemen, at least two-thirds of the goods and services which homes require can be more efficiently produced domestically with electrically-powered tools.[19]

The Goodmans then turn to the fourth of the plans rejected in Russia in 1935, the Soviet regional plan which sought the 'elimination of the difference between the city and the village' through regional decentralisation of industry and industrialisation of agriculture. They perceive that the local self-sufficiency this implies would have led to a kind of syndicalist independence which central dictatorship from Moscow could not tolerate, and they see a logical application of the idea not in the *kolkhoz*, the

Soviet collective farm, but in the *kvutzah* or *kibbutz* in Palestine. (They were writing before the foundation of the state of Israel.)

Finally, as the last of 'the many noble attempts at community' which together form their manual of modern plans the Goodmans consider the Tennessee Valley Authority, whose unique feature, they discern, was 'the decision to spread the benefits of one part of the enterprise, the waterway, to the farmers involved in the total enterprise without specific cash evaluation of the cash outlay and return: the principle is just the general social benefit.' After carefully pinpointing the virtues of this genuinely regional plan, they conclude that the development of the region,

> unlimited though it may be, goes only a short way toward solving community problems, the problems of surplus and leisure, of the relation of culture and work, and the role of great cities. Once a region is electrified, it will eventually become overelectrified, a slum of dynamos and an advertiser's paradise of electrical appliances.

Having described and criticised their miscellany of modern plans, the Goodmans turn to their own, stating their approach in the following terms. (It is worth noting how much more they describe the preoccupations of the 1990s than those of the 1940s.)

> Our concern in this book centres on the following convictions: that the multiplication of commodities and the false standard of living on the one hand, the complication of the economic and technical structure in which one can work at a job on the other hand, and the lack of direct relationship between the two, have by now made a great part of external life morally meaningless. Economic plans to avoid unemployment, to raise the standard of living, to develop backward regions—these are useful, but they do not touch the essential modern problems: the selective use of machine technology, the use of an available surplus, and the distance between means and

ends. The concrete solutions of these problems are community plans. Our concerns are how to make the multitude of goods good for something, how to integrate the work and culture, and how to keep an integrated community plan from becoming a plan for complete slavery.

Emphasising one kind of human aspiration after another, the Goodmans arrive at three completely different community 'paradigms': communities for efficient consumption, for elimination of the difference between production and consumption, and for planned security with minimum regulation. Each is presented in a regional context, though they are not meant to be taken as concrete plans.

In the first place, there is no planning without a physical site and a particular history and population. In the second place, our formulae are extremes and abstractions, but there is no particular place without a mixture. Speaking very broadly, we should say that the first formula is especially applicable to highly industrialised and populous places, the second to places of sparse settlement, new industry and new culture, and the third to old and populous countries, with ancient cultures but relatively little modern technology.

The City of Efficient Consumption is presented as the logical environment of a consumer centred society. Its preliminary conditions are these. A population of several millions is the least economic unit (because the combination of mass production and variety of choice is required, and concentration of the market is the efficient solution to problems of distribution and servicing under conditions of mass production); work and life centre on the market; the moral drives are imitation and emulation; the decoration is display; close by it open country, for full flight.

The centre of the city is developed as one vast air-conditioned cylinder in which (a) the intermediary streets vanish, (b) 'the through driveways now carry out their function to the end, bringing passengers and goods directly to stations in the container, without two speeds and without double loading for trucks and trains', and (c) 'the corridors are transfigured, assuming the functions of promenade and display which thè streets performed so badly. The city has become spacious, with the spaciousness of a great department store.'

Outside the centre is the second ring of buildings, the university, theatres, museums and libraries—the 'region of the things which have been created and discovered but are not consumed in the enjoyment'—and beyond this is the residential zone. We already know its role. 'In the city of efficient consumption, the neighbourhood is the unit of emulation and invidious imputation. This is demonstrated as follows. It is in the end unsatisfactory and indelicate to emulate or impute economic inferiority to one's family and friends: on the other hand, to do so with complete strangers is pointless. Therefore, at least for domestic display, the unit of emulation, etc, must be the neighbourhood.'

Beyond the residential zone is the open country, or 'vacationland', where 'there is exchanged for the existence where everything is done for one, the existence where nothing is done for one'; and beyond this, because such conditions are too hard for city folk, there is, finally—'after fifty miles, which is to say three-quarters of an hour by car on the superhighway or fifteen minutes by helicopter on the beam'—the 'imitation wilderness of state parks and the bathos of adult camps'.

The Goodmans' account of the city of efficient consumption ends with a description of the season of carnival: a saturnalia of fornication, wild destruction, and the remittance of instalment payments, whose principles 'would simply be the satisfaction in the negation of all of the schedules: just as no one can resist a thrill of satisfaction when a blizzard piles up in our streets and everything comes to a standstill.' The social function of the carnival is, of course, to get rid of last year's goods, to wipe out last year's debts to permit new borrowing, and to engender children. But before leaving the city of efficient consumption, something must be said about its politics. The people, explain the authors, exercise no direct political initiative at all:

> Try as one will, it is impossible to discover in an immense and immensely expanding industrialism a loophole where the ordinary man can intervene directly to determine his specific work or the shape of his community life: that is, to decide these matters directly on the basis of his own knowledge and power. The reason is that such an expanding economy exists more and more in its interrelationships, and individual knowledge and, especially, power are less and less adequate... Now an existence of this kind, apparently so repugnant to craftsmen, farmers, artists, and any others who want a say in what they lend their hands to, is nevertheless the existence that is satisfactory to the mass of our countrymen, and therefore it must express deep and universal impulses. These probably centre on what Morris Cohen used to call the first principle of politics—inertia: that is, the fact that people do not want to take the trouble to rule and decide because, presumably, they have more important things to do.'

The City of Efficient Consumption is presented half sardonically, half seriously. If you really want a society in which consumer values are supreme, the authors imply, this is what it should be like.

In their second model, 'The New Commune', the Goodmans seek the elimination of the difference between production and consumption in a decentralised society. They note that garden city plans were based on 'the humane intuition that work in which people have the satisfaction neither of direction nor of wages is essentially unbearable: the worker is eager to be let loose and to go far away.' But they refuse to see the separation of work from the rest of life as immutable: instead, they propose a model in which they are reunited, not by scrapping technology, but by reshaping it closer to human needs:

Starting from the present separation of work and home, we can achieve their closer relation from two sides: (a) returning parts of the production to home workshops or to the proximity of the homes, and (b) introducing domestic work and the productive part of family relations, which are not now considered part of the economy at all, into the style and relations of the larger economy.

Like Kropotkin at the turn of the century—or like Fritz Schumacher or Victor Papanek decades later—the Goodmans seize on the beautiful technical possibilities for decentralisation which the proliferation of tools and new sources of power have brought; and like Ralph Borsodi, they dwell on the economies of small scale and the 'formidable economic value' of home work like cooking, cleaning and child rearing. A chief cause, they observe, of the 'living meaninglessness of industrial work is that each machine worker is acquainted with only a few processes, not with the whole order of production; and, even worse, that the thousands of products are distributed where the worker has no acquaintance at all.'

They ask whether it would not prove more efficient in the long run if people were working for themselves and had a say in the distribution. And they add that 'a say in the distribution' means not merely economic democracy or even socialist ownership. 'These are necessary checks, but they do not give a political meaning to industrialism as such. What is required is the organisation of economic democracy on the basis of the productive units, where each unit, relying on its own expertness and the bargaining power of what it has to offer, cooperates with, and delegates authority to, the whole of society. This is syndicalism. And to guarantee the independent say of each productive unit, it must have a relative self-sufficiency: this is regionalism and the union of farm and factory.'

Diversified farming alone, the Goodmans observe, is economically independent, which is why small farms have always been a root of social stability, though not necessarily of peasant conservatism. On the other hand, taking advantage of mechanisation, such farms can now 'import power and small machines and pay with the products of domestic industry and cash crops farmed perhaps cooperatively with large machines. Such a farm is then the type of productive unit, independent in itself, but linked with the larger economy of the other farms and of the town.' In industry the problem is the reverse, since every machine industry is dependent on the national economy. 'But by regional independence of industries and by the close integration of factory and farm workers—factory hands taking over in the fields at peak seasons, farmers doing factory work in the winter, town people (especially children) living in the country, farmers making small parts for the factories—the industrial region as a whole can secure for itself an independent bargaining power in the national whole.'

They support their case with diagrams of the physical planning of regions on this model, and glimpses of piazzas in the town centres and of 'a farm and its children'—the farmstead being a kind of extended family house plus youth hostel.

But is planning on these lines worthwhile? Or rather, is the formulation of this kind of model for society worth the effort? The authors' answer is this:

> It might be said that all these provisions—small units, double markets, the selection of industries on political and psychological grounds, etc—that all this is a strange and roundabout way of achieving a unified national economy, when at present this unity already exists with a tightness and efficiency that leaves nothing to be desired. But first, it is always a question whether the regional and syndicalist method is not more efficient in the end, when invention, for instance, is not inhibited and the job is its own incentive. But most important of all, it must be remembered that we are here aiming at the highest and nearest ideals of external life: liberty, personal concern, responsiblity and expertness, and a say in

what a man lends his hand to. Compared with these things, the present setup, that does not even make the attempt to find living meaning in work, has nothing to offer.

These last two sentences are the key to this immensely imaginative book: they guarantee its future relevance. But the Goodmans have a third 'paradigm' for us to consider, an interim plan for 'Planned Security with Minimum Regulation'.

Up to about fifty years ago, they say, more than half the productive capacity of industrialised nations was devoted to subsistence. This 'could be regarded as the chief end of the economy and, although their motives were personal wealth and power, most enterprises were concerned with the subsistence market.' But nowadays, less than a tenth of the industrial economy is concerned with subsistence goods (the exact figure depending on where the minimum is set, which is a cultural rather than a medical question), and 'the centre of economic interest has gradually shifted from either providing goods or gaining wealth to keeping the capital machines at work and running at full capacity.' As a result, 'social arrangements have become so complicated and interdependent that, unless the machines are running at full capacity, investment is withdrawn, and all wealth and subsistence are jeopardised.' Since to neglect subsistence and security is seen as 'breeding war and social revolution', governments intervene to assure the elementary security which is no longer the first concern of the economy.

But since the forms and aims of governments are given by the economy rather than by the elementary needs, the tack which they take is the following: to guarantee social security by subsidising the full productivity of the economy. Or to put if financially, security is provided by insurance paid in the money that comes from the operation of the whole economy. The amazing indirectness of this mode of proceeding is brilliantly exposed by the discovery of a new human 'right':

the right—no, not to life and liberty—but to employment! Full employment is the device by which the whole economy can flourish and yet subsistence not be jeopardised—and therefore the curse of Adam becomes a benefit to be struggled for, just because we have the means to produce a surplus, cause of all our woes. But the immediate result of such a solution is to tighten even closer the economic net. Whatever freedom used to come from free enterprise and free markets— a freedom that at one time fought on the side of human rights—is caught in regulation and taxes. In a word, the union of government and economy becomes more and more complete: soon we are in the full tide of statism. This is not a question of evil intention but follows from the connection of the basic political need of subsistence with the totality of an integrated economy. Such is the indirect solution.

The direct solution which the Goodmans suggest is to divide the economy into two, separating whatever provides life and security for all from the rest of the economy, which would continue to provide variety, interest, convenience, emulation, luxury, wealth and power. The principle is to assure subsistence by direct production of subsistence goods and services rather than by insurance taxed on the general economy. This would involve a double money system: the 'hard' money of the subsistence economy and the 'soft' money of the general market. The hard money of the subsistence economy would be more like ration coupons, not negotiable, since 'a man's right to life is not subject to trade.' To the individual, they claim, the separation of his subsistence (employing a small fraction of his labour time) from the demands and values of the general economy (employing most of his labour time) 'should give a breath of freedom, a new possibility of choice, and a sense of security combined with perfect independence, for he has worked directly for what he gets and need never feel the pressure of being a drain on the general society and of thinking that soon the payments will cease.'

The Goodman brothers admit, with a twinge of conscience, that their plan in effect requires a form of industrial conscription for 'universal labour service' in the subsistence economy, even though it would be for only a short period of the individual's working life. 'We are touching,' they remark

on a political principle of vast importance, far beyond our scope of analysis here, namely the principle of purity of means in the exercise of the different powers of modern society. Government, founded essentially on authority, uses mainly the means of personal service: economy, founded essentially on exchange, uses mainly the means of money.' They claim that although their plan is coercive, 'in fact, if not in law, it is less coercive than the situation we are used to. For the great mass of wage earners, it fixes a limit to the coercion to which, between capital and trade union, they are unavoidably and increasingly subjected: and for the wealthy enterpriser, who would buy substitutes, it is no more coercive than any other tax. On constitutional grounds, the crucial objections to forced labour have always been either that it broadens the power of the state in abrogation of the rights against tyranny: but neither of these objections is here valid.'

The minimum subsistence economy (note that if freedom is the goal, everything beyond the minimum must be excluded) would provide and distribute food, clothing and shelter, mass produced in enormous quantities and without variation of style, while medicine and transportation would be provided by a financial arrangement between the subsistence and the general economies. But the Goodman brothers add a warning:

Now supposing that such a system, of assured subsistence and of almost complete freedom of economic ties, were put into effect: there is no doubt that for millions of people, no matter how much they might resist the idea in prospect, the first effect would be a feeling of immense relief—relief from the pressure of daily grind, and from the anxiety of failure: in short, the feeling expressed by so many people that they wish their vacations could last on and on. But, after the first commonplace effect had worn off, then, it seems to us, the moral attitude of people would be profoundly disturbed. They would be afraid not only of freedom (which releases the desires both creative and destructive, which are so nicely repressed by routine), but especially of boredom, for they would imagine themselves completely without cultural or creative resources. For in our times, all entertainment and even the personal excitements of romance seem to be bound up with having ready money to spend: all emotional satisfaction has been intricated into keeping the entire productive machine in motion...

The Goodman brothers enjoy themselves working out the physical implications of their double economy, anticipating much later architectural discussion of the long-life, loose-fit, low-energy philosophy. They also anticipate John Kenneth Galbraith's argument in *The Affluent Society* for 'breaking the connection between security and production'. Echoing the Goodman argument Galbraith remarked that 'We have seen that while our productive energies are used to make things of no great urgency— things for which the demand must be synthesised at elaborate cost or they might not be wanted at all—the process of production continues to be of nearly undiminished urgency as a source of income. The income men derive from producing things of slight consequence is of great consequence. The production reflects the low marginal utility of the goods to society. The income reflects the high total utility of a livelihood to a person.'[20]

Communitas was in fact a book that foreshadowed many later preoccupations of its readers and invited them to conceive alternative solutions for themselves. They might, for example, imagine a triple-decker society in which all three of the Goodman schemes co-exist. Indeed, since one of the fascinations of the book is that the three 'paradigms' are part parodies as well as part utopias, you can actually see them coexisting in a distorting mirror image, in the contemporary world. There are Cities of Efficient Consumption in the out-of-town hypermarkets beyond the cities of the affluent world. Here is a description by the editors of *The Architects' Journal* of the Meadowhall Centre, outside Sheffield:

> It has streets with proper names, like High Street and Park Lane; it has a public square in which crowds of tourists can sit and eat in pavement cafés; it has an equivalent of a local newspaper in the shape of a video wall; it even has its own police force. But don't get too excited, because of course it's all a sham... the districts are just different stage sets, the video wall is sponsored by Coca Cola, and the police force is just a band of security men whose presence is meant to deter any deviance from narrow social norms. And of course, nobody lives there... It denies everything that a town is for. It has no creative mix of functions—just a great slab of retailing plus fast food. It doesn't save energy, it squanders it—the biggest retail car park in the world is hardly going to encourage the use of public transport. It has no government, aside from the autocracy of what Joe Holyoak calls 'corporate centrism'. It allows no expression of community or of individuality. It does not enhance freedom, it diminishes it by sapping the economic lifeblood of real towns.[21]

Similarly the real world has plenty of aspirations for the New Commune. Dennis Hardy explains that

> The record since the 1960s has been two-fold. On the one hand, the decentralist ideas which underpinned the formation of communes have spread outwards to embrace a widening circle of activities, from food co-operatives to green politics. Thus, just beneath the surface of society in Britain today is evolving a whole new fabric that makes up the Alternative

Movement. Ideas (to do, for instance, with the role of women, appropriate technology, and healthy diets) considered marginal if not irrelevant to the interests of mainstream society have now been incorporated in conventional thinking and social behaviour. At the same time, there have been changes within the commune movement itself. Rejection for its own sake has been replaced by a new philosophy, geared to hard work for useful ends, and positive in their approach to new forms of technology and human relationships.[22]

Ironically, it is the third of the Goodman 'paradigms' that has had least appeal, in the very period when the endless productive capacity of the industrial nations made it most feasible. The issue of Maximum Security and Minimum Regulation was one which both American and British governments were concerned with at the very time when they were writing. The mood was one of resolution for a social security system to remove the worst horrors of poverty and insecurity. Elaborate methods were chosen. But by the 1970s and 1980s the conventional wisdom had been put into reverse and in both countries it was thought prudent to increase the incomes of the rich to encourage them to work harder, but at the same time to reduce the incomes of the poor with precisely the same intention. The claiming classes were cheerfully dismissed as the 'underclass'. We are further than ever from Galbraith's recommendation that we should break the connection between income and production, let alone from the Goodman suggestion. All the same we can still see elements of the aim of maximum security and minimum regulation in the lives of the disaffiliated young, living in the interstices of the affluent society by undertaking a minimum of casual, humble, but often useful work, in order to devote the rest of their time to the pursuits of their choice.

There are more ideas to the page in *Communitas* than in any other book I have read. The authors, architect and poet, explained in their original preface that 'the brothers alone can do together what together they could not do separately.' Certainly it contains all the themes that Paul had the chance to develop in half a dozen books on social issues in the 1960s. And certainly the collaboration profoundly affected Percy. He told me in 1973, the year after his brother's death, that their collaboration on this book had been a turning point in his own life. Indeed, in the planning politics of New York, Percy became an increasingly radical critic of what was actually happening, taking part in a sit-down protest against his own university's real-estate imperialism in the neighbourhood and against the speculative onslaught on Harlem. He insisted that his profession was only justified if it served all the people, and not just developers.

But it was Paul who sought to put the planning of human settlements into a framework of ideas. He was, just like Patrick Geddes, years before, a thinker who insisted that the field we choose to call town and country planning was not a profession but a concern of every citizen. He admitted cheerfully that he had been criticised as an ignorant man who spread himself thinly on an endless variety of subjects. but he claimed that his forty or more books had only one subject: 'the human beings I know in their man-made environment'.

References

INTRODUCTION

1 Cassandra in the *Daily Mirror* 15 June 1942
2 Richard Hoggart *A Sort of Clowning, Life and Times 1940-1959* (Chatto and Windus 1990)
3 Comte de Volney *The Ruins, a Survey of the Revolutions of Empires* (London 1797). This book was reprinted in cheap editions well into the present century and was seen as 'the Poor Man's Gibbon'.

Chapter 1: EDUCATION

1 C. Kegan Paul *William Godwin: his Friends and Contemporaries* (Henry S. King 1876)
2 J. Bronowski *William Blake and the Age of Revolution* (Routledge and Kegan Paul 1972)
3 C. Kegan Paul *op cit*
4 William Godwin *The Enquirer. Reflections on Education, Manners and Literature* (G. G. & J. Robinson 1797)
5 C. Kegan Paul *op cit*
6 (Anon) *An Account of the Seminary that will be opened on Monday the Fourth Day of August at Epsom in Surrey* (T. Cadell 1783)
7 William St Clair *The Godwins and the Shelleys* (Faber & Faber 1989)
8 Rosalie Glynn Grylls *William Godwin and his World* (Odhams

1953)

9 H. N. Brailsford *Shelley, Godwin and their Circle* (Williams and Norgate 1913)

10 Claire Tomalin *The Life and Death of Mary Wollstonecraft* (Weidenfeld and Nicolson 1974, Penguin 1977)

11 *ibid*

12 William Godwin *Memoirs of the Author of the Rights of Woman* (J. Johnson and G. G. & J. Robinson 1798, Penguin Classics 1987)

13 Claire Tomalin *op cit*

14 William Godwin *op cit*

15 Mary Wollstonecraft *Vindication of the Rights of Woman* (J. Johnson 1792, Penguin Classics 1982)

16 Thomas Paine *Common Sense* (1776, J. Johnson 1792)

17 William Godwin *An Enquiry Concerning Political Justice, and its Influence on General Virtue and Happiness* (G. G. & J. Robinson 1793, 1796, 1798, Penguin Classics 1976)

18 cited with other examples in Colin Ward *The Child in the Country* (Bedford Square Press 1989)

19 Colin Ward 'What is going to happen yesterday?' *Times Educational Supplement* 31 March 1989, 'Put the class before the forms' *The Times* 10 October 1990

20 Mary Wollstonecraft *Letters Written During a Short Residence in Sweden, Norway and Denmark* (J. Johnson 1796, Penguin Classics 1987)

21 Richard Holmes 'Introduction ' to the above, edited together with Godwin's *Memoirs of the Author of the Rights of Woman.*

22 William St Clair *The Godwins and the Shelleys: The biography of a family* (Faber & Faber 1989); Janet Todd (ed) *A Wollstonecraft Anthology* (Polity Press 1989)

23 this, and subsequent quotations, unless shown otherwise, are from William Godwin *The Enquirer, Reflections on Education, Manners and Literature* (G. G. & J. Robinson 1797)

24 David Wills *Throw Away Thy Rod: Living with difficult children* (Gollancz 1960)

25 W. David Wills *The Barns Experiment* (Allen & Unwin 1945)
26 Paul and Jean Ritter *The Free Family* (Gollancz 1959)
27 William Godwin *Memoirs of the Author of the Rights of Woman* (2nd edition, J. Johnson and G. G. & J. Robinson, 1798)
28 *ibid*

Chapter 2: POLITICS

1 Richard Holmes: Introduction to Mary Wollstonecraft *A Short Residence in Sweden*, and William Godwin *Memoirs of the Author of The Rights of Women* (Penguin Classics 1987)
2 Isaiah Berlin: Introduction to Alexander Herzen *From the Other Shore* and *The Russian People and Socialism*, trans. by Moura Budberg (Weidenfeld and Nicolson 1956, Oxford Paperbacks 1979)
3 E. H. Carr *Michael Bakunin* (Macmillan 1937, paperback 1966)
4 Martin Malia *Alexander Herzen and the Birth of Russian Socialism* (Harvard 1961)
5 E. H. Carr *The Romantic Exiles: A Nineteenth-Century Portrait Gallery* (1933, Penguin 1949)
6 Isaiah Berlin 'A Marvellous Decade', Encounter June 1955, Nov 1955, Dec 1955 and May 1956, reprinted as 'A Remarkable Decade' in Isaiah Berlin *Russian Thinkers* (Hogarth Press 1978)
7 Alexander Herzen *From the Other Shore, op cit*
8 Marc Slonim *The Epic of Russian Literature* (Oxford University Press 1950)
9 See for example Michael Bakunin *Marxism, Freedom and the State*, ed. by K. J. Kenafick (Freedom Press 1950, 1990); Michael Bakunin *Selected Writings*, ed. Arthur Lehning (Jonathan Cape 1973)
10 Henri Troyat *Tolstoy* (W. H. Allen 1968, Penguin 1970)
11 Alexander Herzen 'Letters to an old comrade' in *My Past and Thoughts*, ed. by Humphrey Higgens (Chatto & Windus, 4 vols, 1968)

Chapter 3: ECONOMICS

1 M. A. Novomeysky *My Siberian Life* (Max Parrish 1976)
2 Peter Kropotkin *Memoirs of a Revolutionist* (Smith Elder 1899)
3 Paul Goodman 'Introduction' to Kropotkin's *Memoirs of a Revolutionist* (Reprinted by Horizon Press 1969)
4 Alexander Solzhenitsyn *August 1914* (Hamish Hamilton 1972)
5 Alexander Berkman *The Bolshevik Myth* (Boni and Liveright 1925, Pluto Press 1989)
  Emma Goldman *My Disillusionment in Russia* (C. W. Daniel 1925, Crowell 1970)
  Emma Goldman *Living My Life* (Alfred A. Knopf 1931, New American Library 1977)
6 Kropotkin's letters to Lenin are printed in Paul Avrich (ed) *The Anarchists in the Russian Revolution* (Thames & Hudson 1973)
7 Lewis Mumford *The City in History* (Penguin 1963)
8 Peter Kropotkin *Fields, Factories and Workshops* (Hutchinson 1899, Allen & Unwin 1974, Freedom Press 1985)
9 Peter Kropotkin, postscript to Russian edition of *Words of a Rebel* (Petrograd and Moscow 1921), translated by Nicolas Walter for a forthcoming English edition of this book.
10 Camillo Berneri *Peter Kropotkin: His Federalist Ideas* (Freedom Press 1943)

Chapter 4: SOCIETY

1 Obituary in *The Guardian* 14 June 1965
2 Television interview with Vernon Sproxton, *The Listener* 18 April 1962
3 This lecture was printed as Martin Buber: 'What is common to all' *The Review of Metaphysics* March 1958
4 Herbert Read *Anarchy and Order: Essays in politics* (Faber 1953)
  Martin Buber *Paths in Utopia* (Routledge & Kegan Paul 1949)
5 Arthur A. Cohen *Martin Buber* (Bowes & Bowes 1957)

6 *ibid*
7 Martin Buber *Israel and Palestine* (East and West Library 1951)
8 Cohen *op cit*
9 Martin Buber *Pointing the Way* (Routledge & Kegan Paul 1957)
10 *Paths in Utopia op cit*
11 *ibid*
12 *ibid*
13 Maurice Friedman *Martin Buber: The Life of Dialogue*
14 (Routledge & Kegan Paul 1955)
   Martin Buber 'Society and the State' *World Review* May 1951,
15 reprinted in *Pointing the Way, op cit*
16 *ibid*

Chapter 5: ARCHITECTURE

1 David Watkin *Architecture and Morality* (Oxford University Press 1978)
2 John McKean *Learning from Segal* (Basel: Birkhauser Verlag 1989)
3 Esther Wood, quoted in Godfrey Rubens *William Richard Lethaby: His Life and Work* (Architectural Press 1986)
4 Stephen Bayley 'W R Lethaby and the cell of tradition' *Royal Institute of British Architects Journal* April 1975
5 John Brandon-Jones interviewed in John McKean *op cit*
6 W. R. Lethaby *Form in Civilisation* (Oxford University Press 1922, reprinted 1937. New edition introd. by Lewis Mumford MIT Press 1957)
7 In C. B. Purdom (ed) *Town Theory and Practice* (Benn 1921)
8 Alfred Powell produced a privately-printed collection of them under the title *Scrips and Scraps*. He also published a selection in *The Times Literary Supplement* in April 1953. The most complete collection is in A. R. N. Roberts (ed) *William Richard Lethaby 1857-1931* (London County Council Central School

of Arts and Crafts 1957)

9 Ralph Freedman *Hermann Hesse: Pilgrim of Crisis* (Jonathan Cape 1979)

10 Walter Segal 'Into the Twenties' *Architectural Review* January 1974

11 Walter Segal 'Timber Framed Housing' *RIBA Journal* July 1977

12 Walter Segal in the *Architectural Review, op cit*

13 Peter Blundell Jones in *The Architects' Journal* 4 May 1988

14 Walter Segal *Home and Environment* (Leonard Hill 1948)

15 Walter Segal 'View from a lifetime' *Transactions of the RIBA Vol 1, 1982*

16 *ibid*

Chapter 6: PLANNING

1 See my Preface to John F. C. Turner *Housing by People* (Marion Boyars 1976)

2 John Turner 'The re-education of a professional' in John F. C. Turner and Robert Fichter (eds) *Freedom to Build: Dweller Control in the Housing Process* (Collier-Macmillan 1972)

3 Lewis Mumford 'The Disciple's Rebellion' *Encounter* September 1966

4 Lewis Mumford *Technics and Civilisation* (Routledge & Kegan Paul 1934), and *The Future of Technics and Civilisation* (Freedom Press 1986)

5 Paddy Kitchen *A Most Unsettling Person* (Gollancz 1975)

6 Philip Mairet *Pioneer of Sociology: Life and Letters of Sir Patrick Geddes* (Lund Humphries 1957)

7 *ibid*

8 Peter Green, Introduction to Patrick Geddes *City Development, A Report to the Carnegie Dunfirmline Trust* (Irish University Press 1973)

9 Patrick Geddes *Urban Improvements: A strategy for Urban Works* (Government of Pakistan Planning Commission 1965)

10 Patrick Geddes *Cities in Evolution* (1915, Williams and Norgate 1949)

11 Jacqueline Tyrwhitt (ed) *Patrick Geddes in India* (Lund Humphries 1947)

12 *ibid*

13 quoted by John Turner *op cit*

14 Philip Boardman *The Worlds of Patrick Geddes* (Routledge & Kegan Paul 1978)

15 *ibid*

16 Peter Hall *Cities of Tomorrow: An Intellectual History of Urban Planning and Design in the Twentieth Century* (Basil Blackwell 1988)

17 Paul Goodman *Art and Social Nature* (Greenberg 1946), reprinted in Taylor Stoehr (ed) *Drawing the Line: The Political Essays of Paul Goodman* (Free Life Editions 1977)

18 Taylor Stoehr 'Rereading Paul Goodman in the Nineties' *Dissent*, Fall 1990

19 Paul and Percival Goodman *Communitas: Ways of Livelihood and Means of Life*, 2nd edition (Vintage Books 1960).
All subsequent quotations from this book are from the 1st edition (University of Chicago Press 1947)

20 John Kenneth Galbraith *The Affluent Society* (Houghton-Mifflin 1958)

21 'Pseudo Town', Editorial in *The Architects' Journal* 21 November 1990

22 Dennis Hardy 'The Anarchist Alternative: a history of community experiments in Britain' *Contemporary Issues in Geography and Education* Vol 3 No 2, 1990

Read for Yourself:
A Bibliographical Appendix

I am a propagandist and I would like the people who have influenced me to influence you too. You will have been able to judge from my copious quotations whether they speak your language. Be warned that my own use of them, like anyone else's, is partial and one-sided. I list here the books by or about them that you are likely to come across in bookshops and libararies.

WILLIAM GODWIN and MARY WOLLSTONECRAFT

Enquiry Concerning Political Justice, edited by Isaak Kramnick, is available as a Penguin Classic (1976). This is the text of the 3rd edition of 1798. If you want to compare editions you have to refer to the facsimile of the 3rd edition with variant readings of the 1st and 2nd editions, edited by F. E. L. Priestley (3 Vols, University of Toronto Press 1946)

The Enquirer. You are not likely to find this. A facsimile reprint exists (Augustus M. Kelley, New York 1965, in a series of Reprints of Economic Classics). Similarly Godwin's other educational writings have appeared from various American university presses. For details see modern biographies.

The best of these is Peter H. Marshall (Yale University Press 1984) George Woodcock's pioneering re-assessment *William Godwin, A Biographical Study* is in print again from Black Rose Books, Montréal (distributed in Britain by Freedom Press).

Peter Marshall has also edited *The Anarchist Writings of William Godwin* (Freedom Press 1986), an attractive and cheap selection.

Mary Wollstonecraft's *Vindication of the Rights of Woman*, edited by Miriam Brody Kramnick is a Penguin Classic (1982). So is Mary Wollstonecraft's *A Short Residence in Sweden*, together with Godwin's *Memoirs of the Author of the Rights of Woman*. Their editor, Richard Holmes, suggests that, considered as literature, these are the best books that either wrote, and he has the best of all possible motives, for he explains that 'In re-publishing them together, as I have long wished, I hope to do their authors honour and to give the causes they believed in and fought for, a more complex and vivid life in the mind of the modern readers they have always deserved.' (Penguin Classics 1987)

After Mary Wollstonecraft's death, Godwin gathered together the *Posthumous Works of the Author of a Vindication of the Rights of Woman* (4 volumes, J. Johnson 1798). Most of them were never reprinted until recently. In 1977 Janet Todd edited her *A Wollstonecraft Anthology* (Indiana University Press 1977, Polity Press 1989). Finally in 1989 *The Complete Works of Mary Wollstonecraft*, edited by Marilyn Butler and Janet Todd, appeared in six volumes. (Pickering 1989, £245.00). Obviously you will never buy this collection, but readers might be inclined to make a series of pilgrimages to their nearest university library.

For both William and Mary and their families there is a book of intense literary detection, William St Clair's *The Godwins and the Shelleys: The Biography of a Family* (Faber & Faber 1989, paperback 1990). This is certainly an absorbing book, and it actually has Appendix I, complete with a table, charting the nights when William and Mary copulated.

But I can't help thinking that it would have been more interesting to chart the mutual influences in the educational thinking of these two pioneers.

ALEXANDER HERZEN

You could spend a happy year's reading time working your way through Herzen's *My Past and Thoughts*, in the 4-volume edition edited by Humphrey Higgens (Chatto & Windus, 4 vols, 1968).

If you can't spare that amount of library visits, there are luckily several readily obtainable paperback selections. One is *Childhood, Youth and Exile*, translated by J. D. Duff and introduced by Isaiah Berlin (World's Classics Paperbacks, OUP 1980). Another is *Ends and Beginnings*, a selection from the rest of the book (OUP Paperbacks 1985). The third is Alexander Herzen: *From the Other Shore* and *The Russian People and Socialism*, translated by Moura Budberg (Oxford Paperbacks 1979).

PETER KROPOTKIN

There are many editions of Kropotkin's *Memoirs of a Revolutionist*. I bought the most recent paperback (edited by James Allen Rogers, The Cresset Library, Century Hutchinson 1988) for £1.99 at Dillons in a remainder sale within a year of publication. So it just depends on where you shop. The best by far is the one edited by Nicolas Walter (Dover Press 1970), due for re-issue. Most of his other books are either published or handled by the publishing house of which Kropotkin was founder, Freedom Press, 84b Whitechapel High Street, London E1 7QX. They include *Mutual Aid*, with an introduction by John Hewetson, and *Fields, Factories and Workshops*, in an edition in which I attempted to bring his arguments up to date.

There are two biographies. One is *The Anarchist Prince* by George Woodcock and Ivan Avakumovic (Boardman 1951, available once more in an edition from Black Rose Books). The other is *Kropotkin* by Martin A. Miller (University of Chicago Press 1976).

MARTIN BUBER

Buber's books, including those which record his social thought, tend to be shelved in bookshops and libraries in the section labelled Religion. From my point of view the ones to look for are *Paths in Utopia* (Routledge & Kegan Paul 1949, Schocken Paperbacks 1965), and *Pointing the Way* (Routledge & Kegan Paul 1957, Harper & Row 1966). A convenient presentation of his thought as a whole is Will Herberg (ed) *The Writings of Martin Buber* (Meridian Books 1955). I'm still looking for Bernard Susser's *Essence and Utopia: Social and Political Thought of Martin Buber* (Dickinson UP, 1981).

W. R. LETHABY

The book you are most likely to find is Godfrey Rubens *William Richard Lethaby: His Life and Work* (Architectural Press 1986). Another absorbing volume is the book produced to accompany the exhibition of 1984 at the Central School of Art and Design: Sylvia Backemeyer and Theresa Gronberg (eds) *W. R. Lethaby 1857-1931, Architecture, Design and Education* (Lund Humphries 1984).

It is worth looking in secondhand bookshops for his little book *Form in Civilisation* (OUP 1922, MIT Press 1957).

WALTER SEGAL

The key book about Walter Segal is John McKean *Learning from Segal*. This is in both English and German, published by Birkhauser Verlag of Basel in 1989. It is obtainable in architectural bookshops, (e.g. the RIBA Bookshop at 66 Portland Place in London, and the bookshop in the basement of the Architectural Association in Bedford Square, London).

There is an excellent account of Segal's approach, together with technical details of his housing 'method', in Brian Richardson and Jon Broome *The Self-Build Book: How to enjoy designing and building your own home* (Green Books 1991).

Segal's work is also being propagated by the Walter Segal Self Build Trust, Room 212, Panther House, 38 Mount Pleasant, London WC1X 0AP.

PATRICK GEDDES

There are more books about Geddes than by him. They all turn up in the second-hand market, and are as follows: Amelia Defries *The Interpreter Geddes: The Man and His Gospel* (Routledge 1927); Philip Boardman *Patrick Geddes: Maker of the Future* (Univ of North Carolina Press 1944); Philip Mairet *Pioneer of Sociology: The Life and Letters of Sir Patrick Geddes* (Lund Humphries 1957); Paddy Kitchen *A Most Unsettling Person: An Introduction to the Ideas and Life of Patrick Geddes* (Gollancz 1975); Philip Boardman *The Worlds of Patrick Geddes: Biologist, Town Planner, Re-educator, Peace Warrior* (Routledge & Kegan Paul 1978).

Which one of these you read is a matter of chance. If I were asked to recommend just one it would be the one by Paddy Kitchen, or for comprehensiveness, the more recent of Philip Boardman's two books. However, there is a new and excellent study, readily available if only you or the library could afford it. This is Helen Meller *Patrick Geddes: Social Evolutionist and City Planner* (Routledge 1990).

PAUL GOODMAN

Whatever happened to all those reprints of *Communitas* in the Vintage Books edition that were floating around in the 1960s? I can never find one in my attempts to pass the book on to other people. It must be a good sign that the books' owners don't want to part with them.

But literally as I write, I learn from America that a new edition is about to appear. This is Paul and Percival Goodman *Communitas* (a Morningside Book from Columbia University Press 1990, in cloth and paperback; the latter costs $14). Some British dealer is bound to import it.

It has an Afterword: 'Communitas Revisited', extracted from Percival Goodman's book *The Double E* (Doubleday Anchor 1988), an exposition of the themes of Economy and Ecology, which he tried to persuade his fellow architects were the key issues for the coming century. Percy sought with delightful and profound humour to pick up the threads of the fraternal discourse of earlier years.

Paul, just like William Godwin, was the subject of a period of 'sultry and unwholesome popularity', when a dozen of his books became available as cheap Vintage paperbacks, distributed in Britain by Wildwood House in 1970. The ones which gratified him most were the re-issues of his stories, novels and poems. The ones I was most delighted to see were his books of social criticism like *Growing Up Absurd* and *Utopian Essays and Practical Proposals*.

Since Paul Goodman's death, Taylor Stoehr has worked very hard to keep his ideas in print, editing one volume after another, including the *Collected Poems* (Random House 1972), four books of the *Collected Stories* (Black Sparrow Press, Santa Barbara 1978-1980) and three books of essays. These are *Drawing the Line* (political essays), *Nature Heals* (psychological essays), and *Creator Spirit Come!* (literary essays), published by Free Life Editions, New York in 1977. There is yet another Goodman book around somewhere. This is *Little Prayers and Finite Experiences* (Harper and Row 1972, Wildwood House 1973).

A Last Word

Paul Goodman inevitably leads me to a final reflection in my shopping-bag of influences. In his very last article he remarked that

> For me, the chief principle of anarchism is not freedom but autonomy, the ability to initiate a task and do it one's own way... The weakness of 'my' anarchism is that the lust for freedom is a powerful motive for political change, whereas autonomy is not. Autonomous people protect themselves stubbornly but by less strenuous means, including plenty of passive resistance. They do their own thing anyway. The pathos of oppressed people, however, is that, if they break free, they don't know what to do. Not having been autonomous, they don't know what it's like, and before they learn, they have new managers who are not in a hurry to abdicate...

I can't think of any reflection more apposite to our dilemmas at the end of the century. And when I look back at my anthology of influences, I find that they all say the same thing. The more sinister aspect of my experience is that all my life I have met plenty of people who decried the usefulness of literacy. Invariably they are highly educated people. They may despise the people who influence them. I cherish the ones who influenced me.